In the COUNTRY of PLASTIC

Photos & Stories

CATHRYN WELLNER

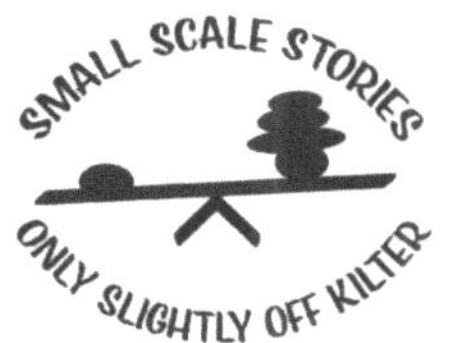

Small Scale Stories #6

Espoir Press

British Columbia 2017

Espoir Press
1002 - 1128 Sunset Drive
Kelowna, British Columbia
Canada V1Y 9W7

In the Country of Plastic (Small Scale Stories #6)

ISBN 978-1-988760-09-4

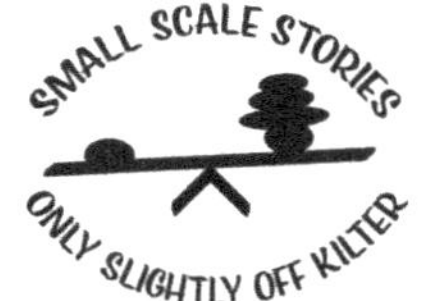

LOVE LETTERS

One summer an osprey pair incorporated a big plastic bag into their nest. It flapped away all summer, like the flag on a pirate ship. The osprey did not seem to mind, though it must have rustled mightily in strong winds.

When they left, a great blue heron used their platform as a resting spot. He, too, seemed unfazed by the plastic bag.

Unfortunately, the planet is fazed by plastic, a lot. Plastic bits attract birds, then clog their bellies. Toxic chemicals leach into streams. Castoffs pile high on beaches, streets and landfills.

Plastic is everywhere and incredibly useful. We wear it, drive in it, and cook with it. Then we throw it away, to slowly degrade even into the food we eat.

And yet, this gorgeous planet keeps giving us gifts like the ones in this book. So kick back and enjoy these small scale stories. They are love letters to this beautiful world that somehow cherishes us in spite of our plastic and our carelessness.

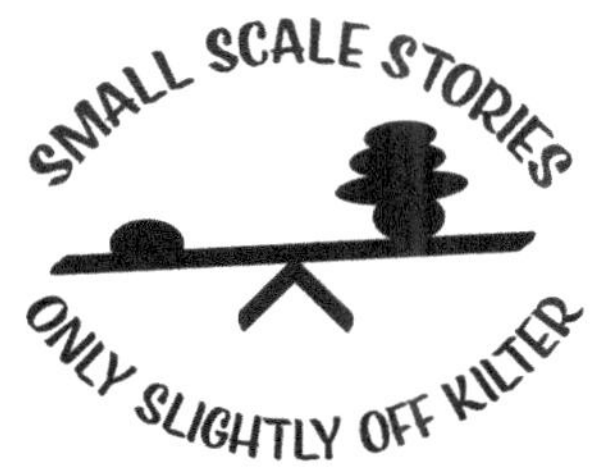

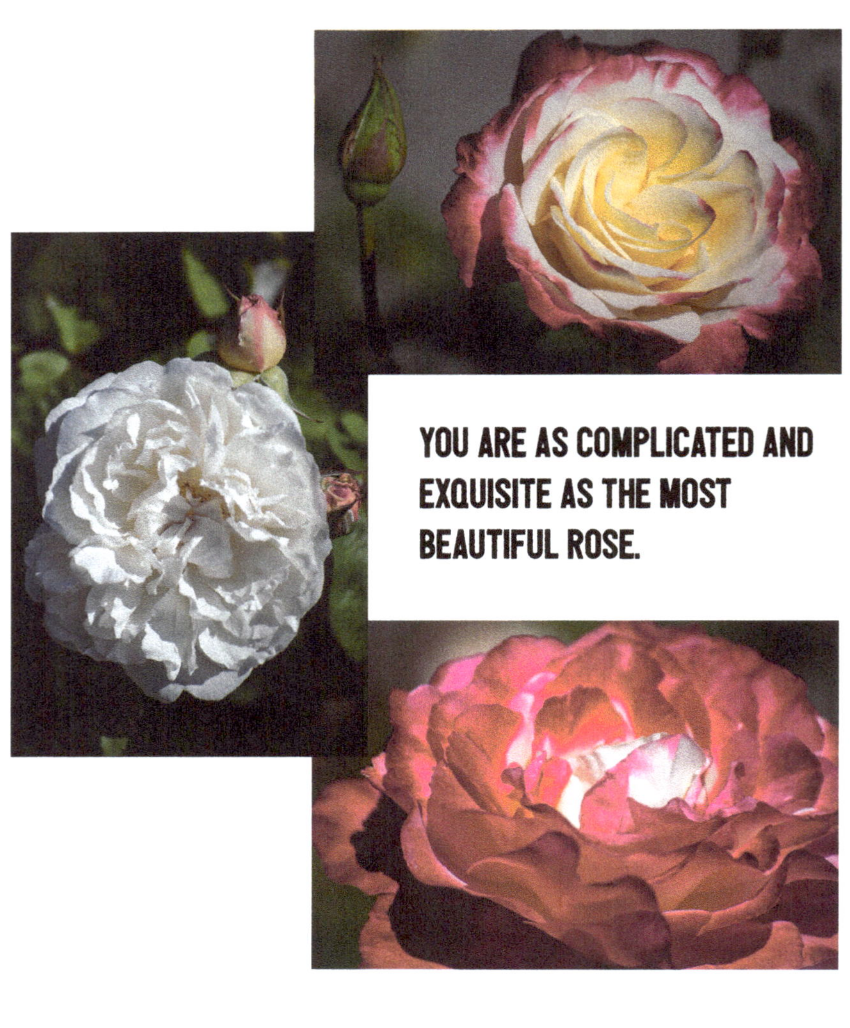
YOU ARE AS COMPLICATED AND
EXQUISITE AS THE MOST
BEAUTIFUL ROSE.

Take time out to

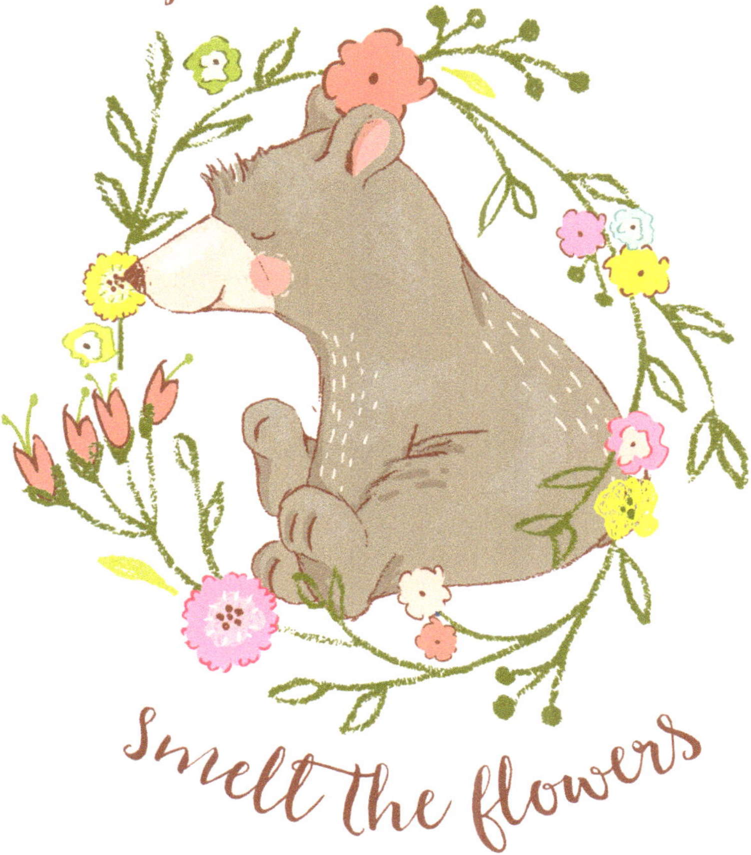

smelt the flowers

THE STORIES

1 Flying the Plastic Flag
2 Alert Deer
3 Adolescent Seeds
4 Awed Watcher
5 Bindweed Life
6 Contented Turtle
7 Bizarre Stories
8 Ducky Mothers
9 Family Reunion
10 Coyote Dinner
11 Gadwall Romeo
12 Good Fisher
13 Uncertain Futures
14 Different Games
15 Disastrous Singing Party
16 Crow Camouflage
17 Glowing Maple
18 Fish Teasing
19 Goose Regrets
20 Generations
21 Killdeer Alarm
22 Slider's Favorite Days
23 Grateful Flowers
24 Handsome Blackbird
25 Small And Purple
26 Hurry, Spring
27 Gull's Beautiful Song
28 Hydrant Plays Snoopy
29 Introvert's Dilemma
30 Radical Radishes
31 Condo's Reflection
32 Stunning Dancer
33 Stone Romeo
34 Scornful Teen
35 Sweet Rain
36 Farewell Waves

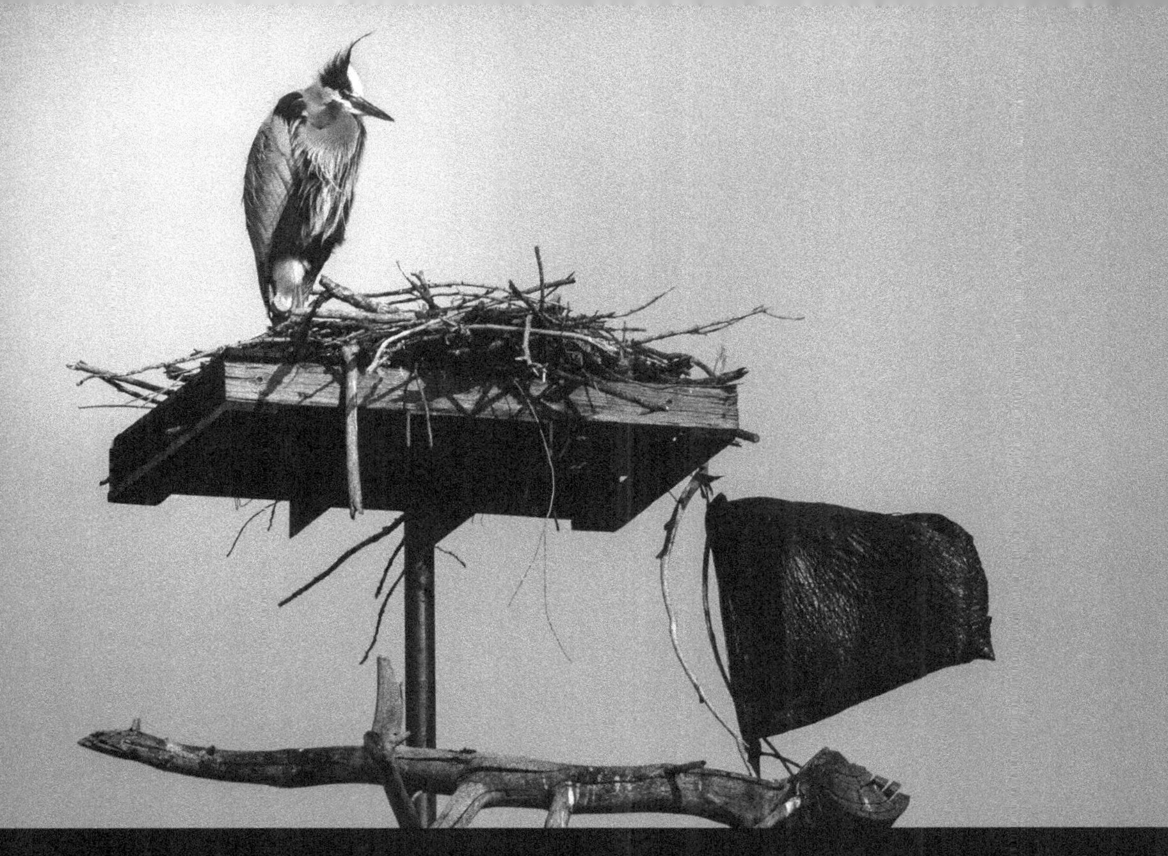

He stood serene and confident, paying no attention to the flapping flag of the humans' Country of Plastic.

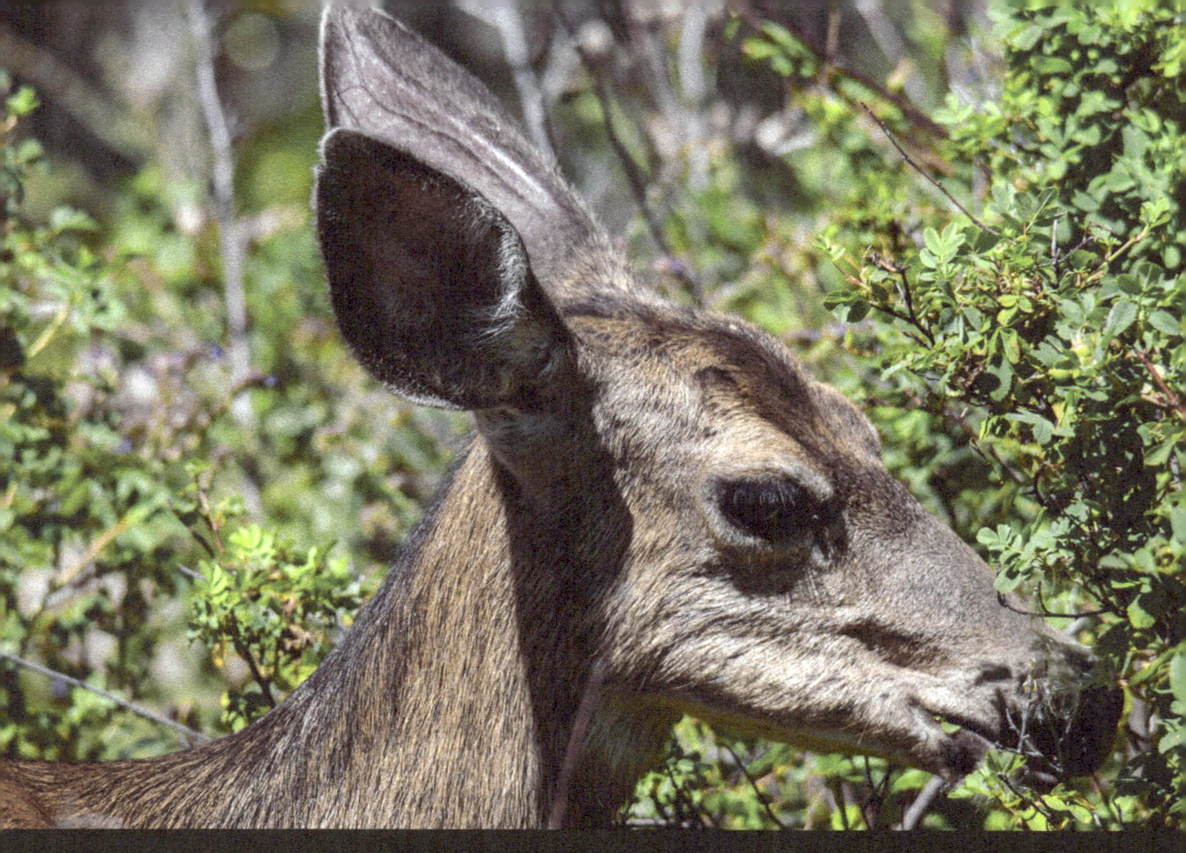

She munched her way through the rose leaves, filling the body that filled the hungry mouth of her fawn. Although she appeared unfazed by the watching humans, she was aware of every movement they made.

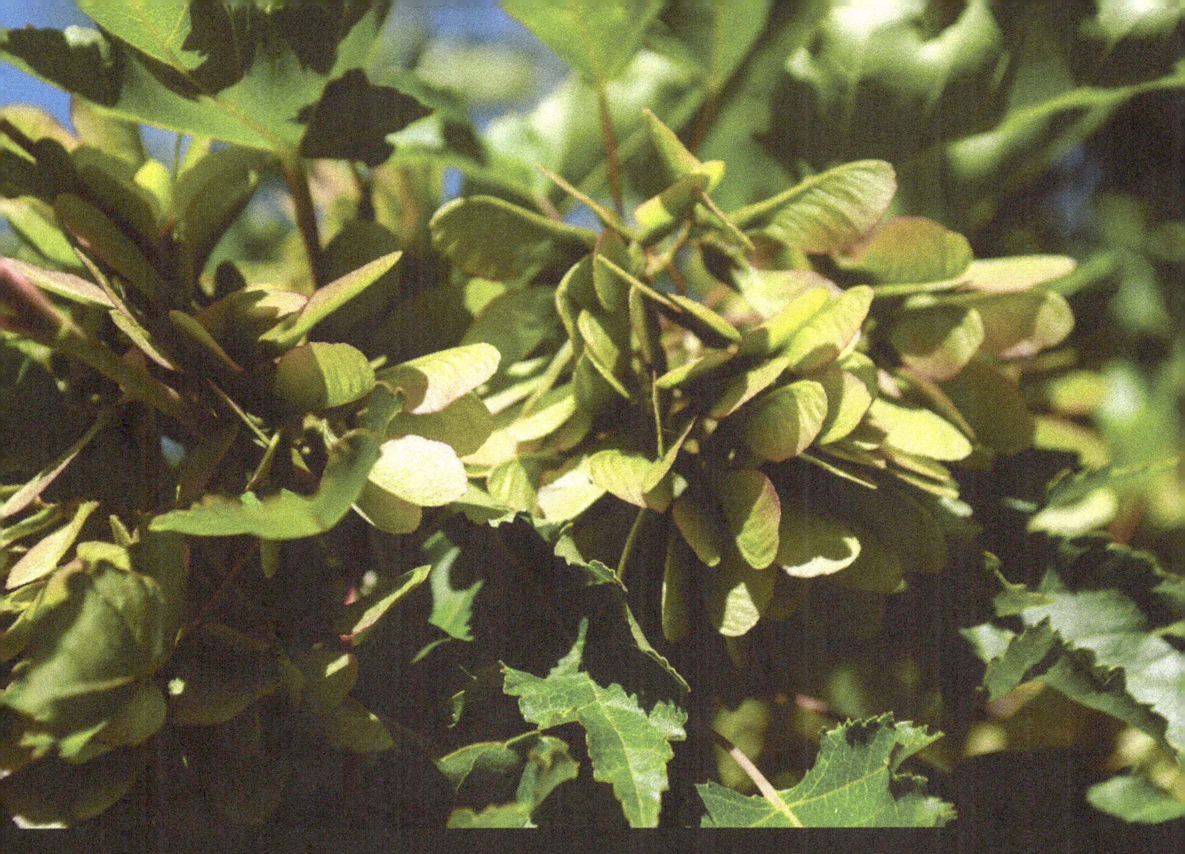

The seed clusters were in the peak of exuberant youth. All they wanted was to be together and enjoy the same parties. By the time the weather changed, they would be ready to say goodbye and fly solo into the unknown.

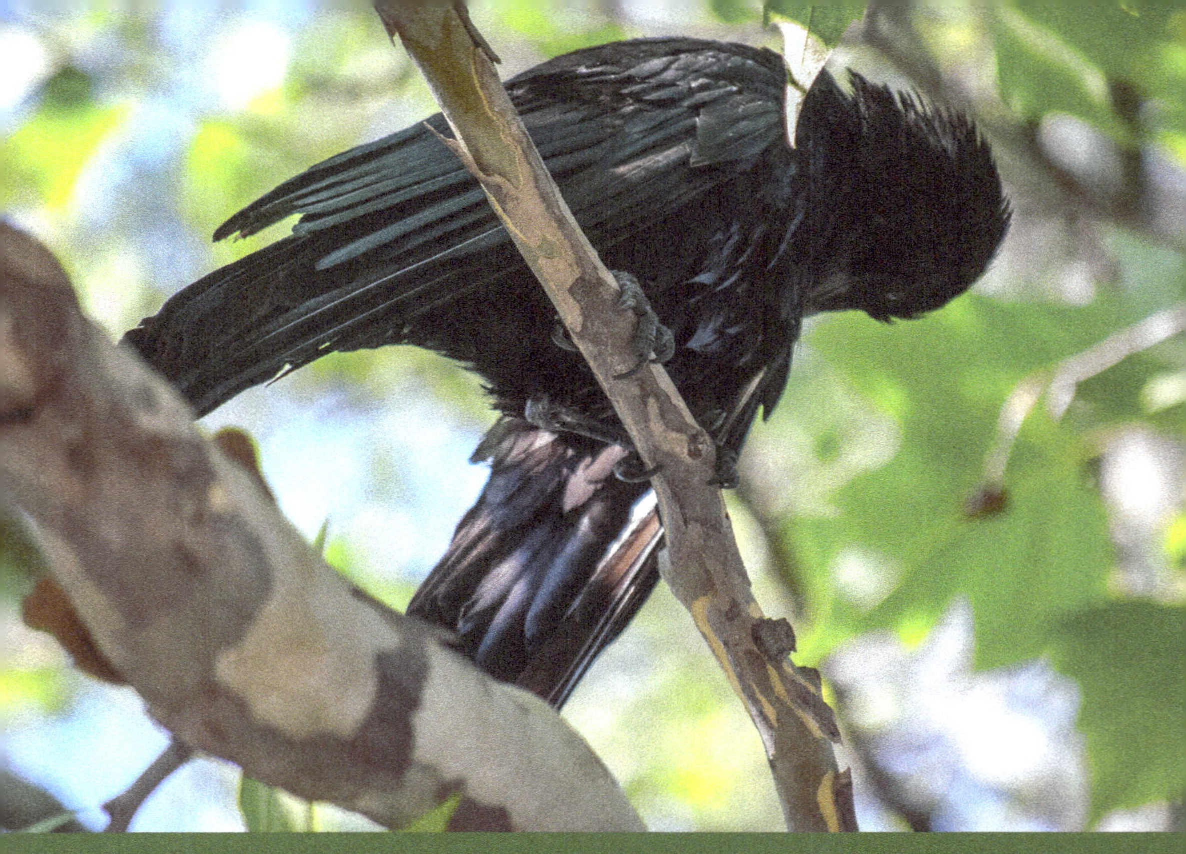

Had he sensed the quiet admiration beaming his way, he would have flown off. Instead, he went about his life, oblivious to the awe of the watcher.

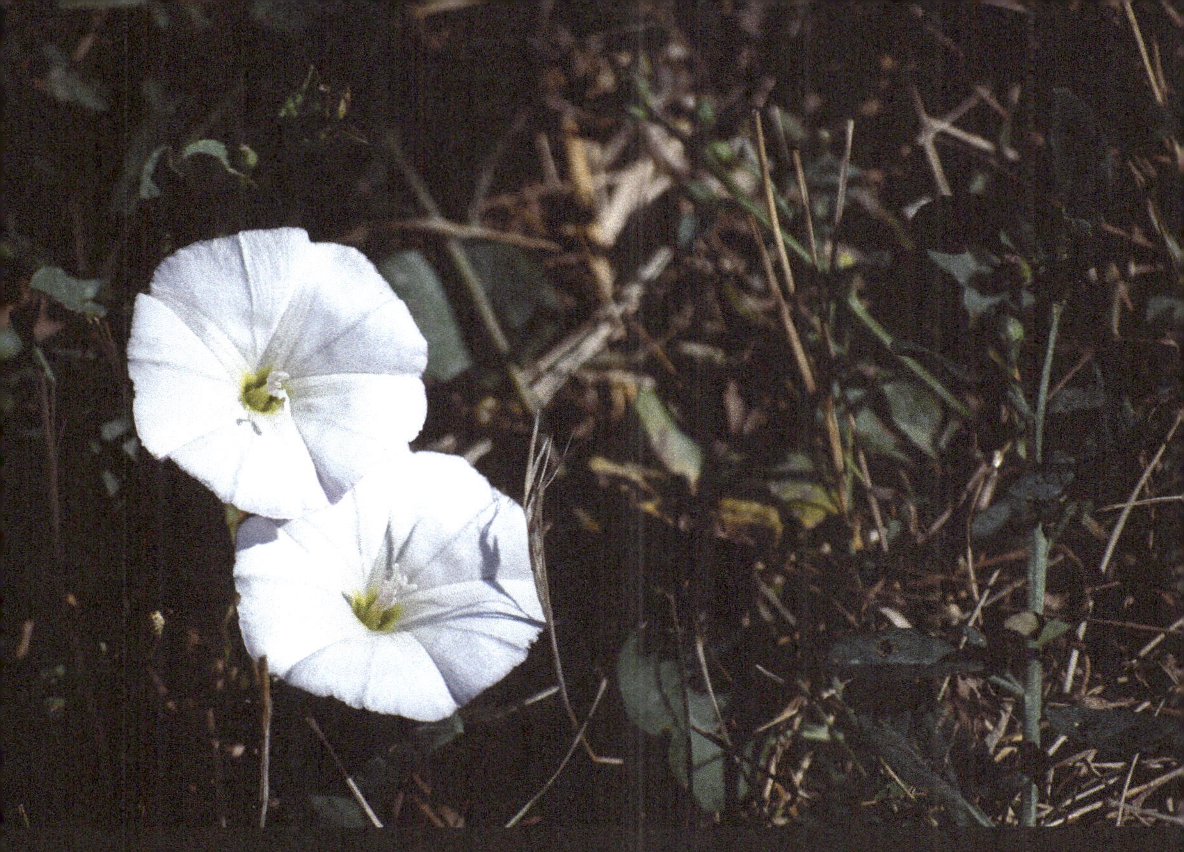

No matter how gloriously bindweed bloomed, no matter how far and generously she spread, the humans loathed her. When they left her alone, her life was an explosion of growth and fun.

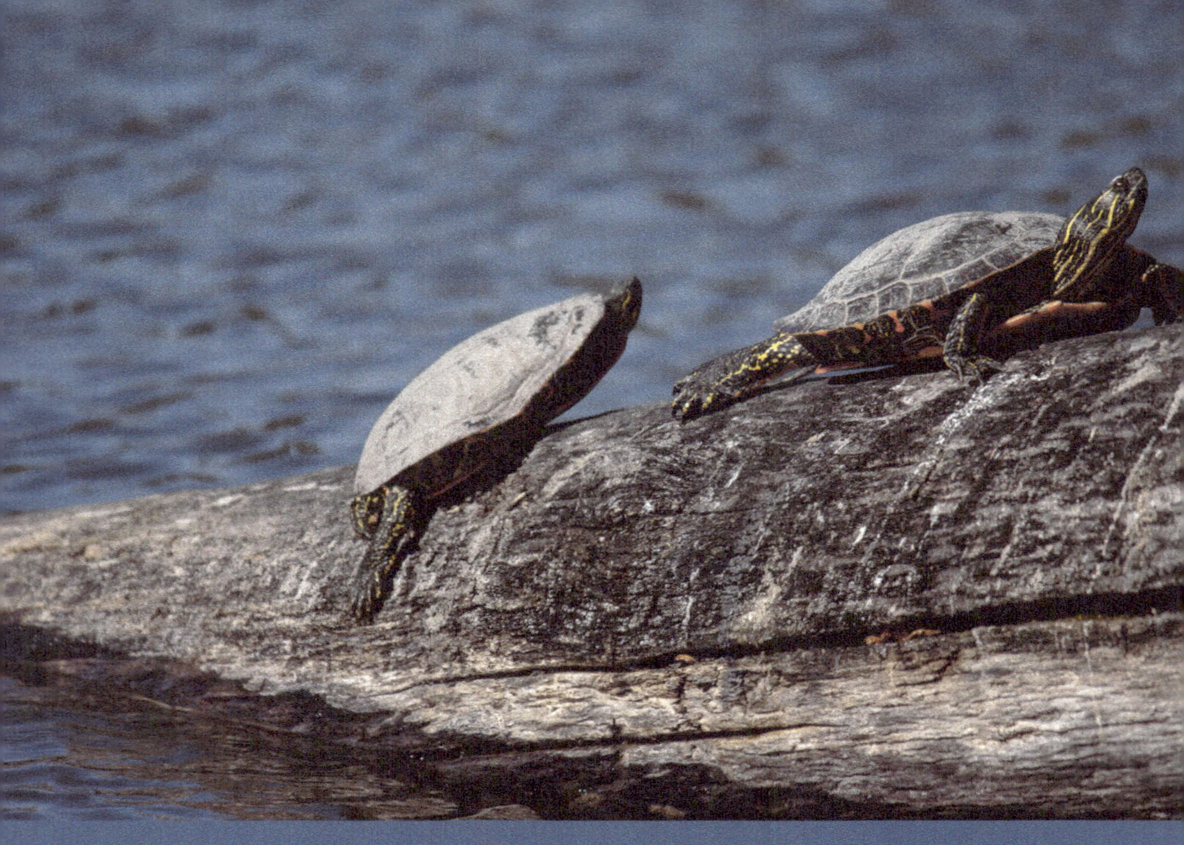

"What's beyond the pond?" asked Curious Turtle.

"Nothing," replied his contented friend. "All we could ever want or need is right here."

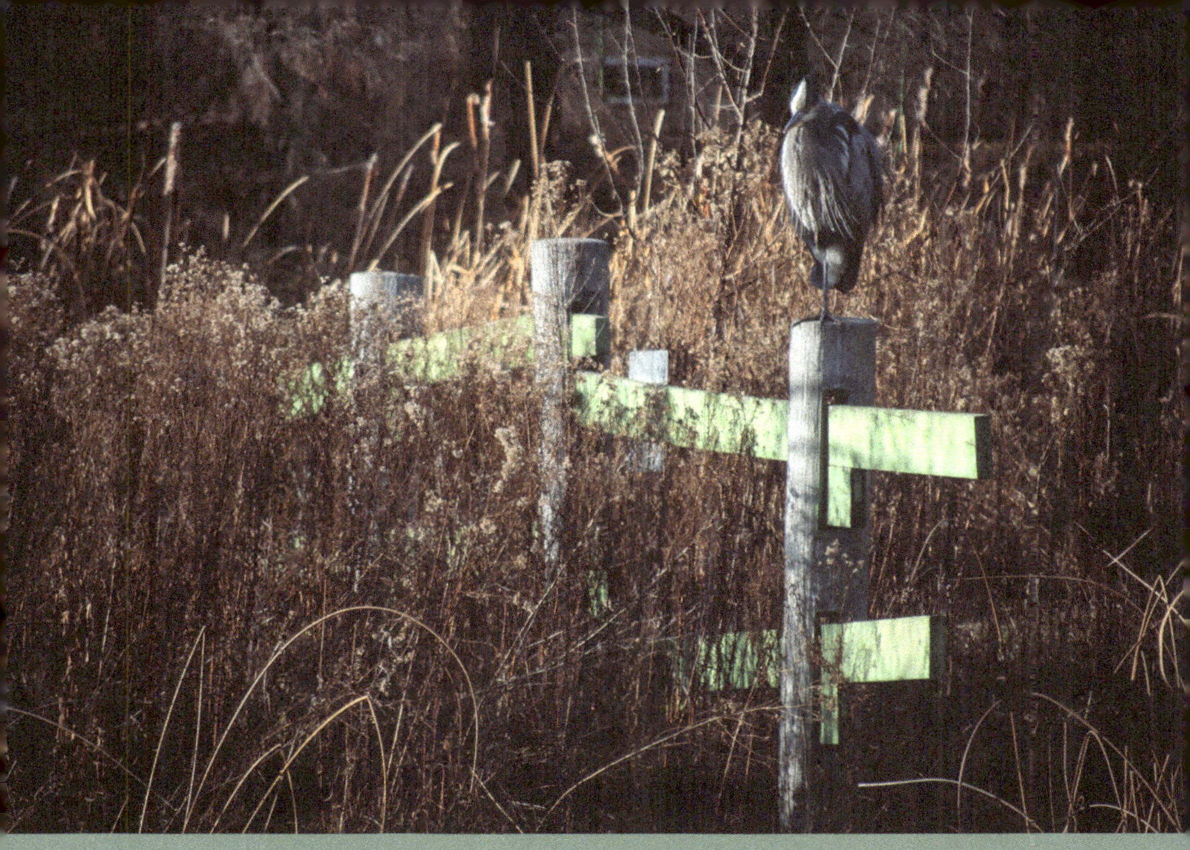

Great Blue Heron chuckled. The watchers speculated as to why he had only one leg. They would be gone before he put his other leg down and would tell bizarre stories about him.

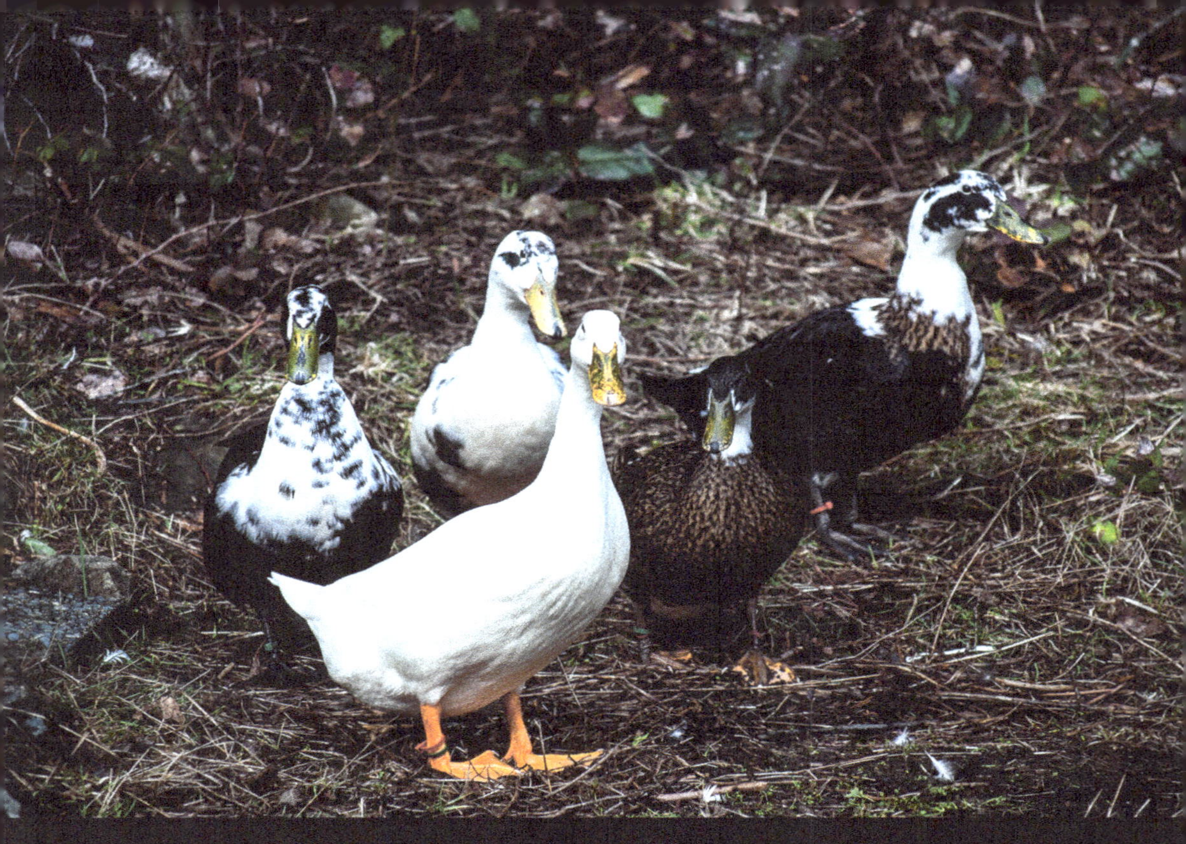

The human was making a strange sound that sounded like "be kind to your web-footed friends, for a duck may be somebody's mother." Who was she kidding? If she kept stealing their eggs, they'd never be any duck's mother.

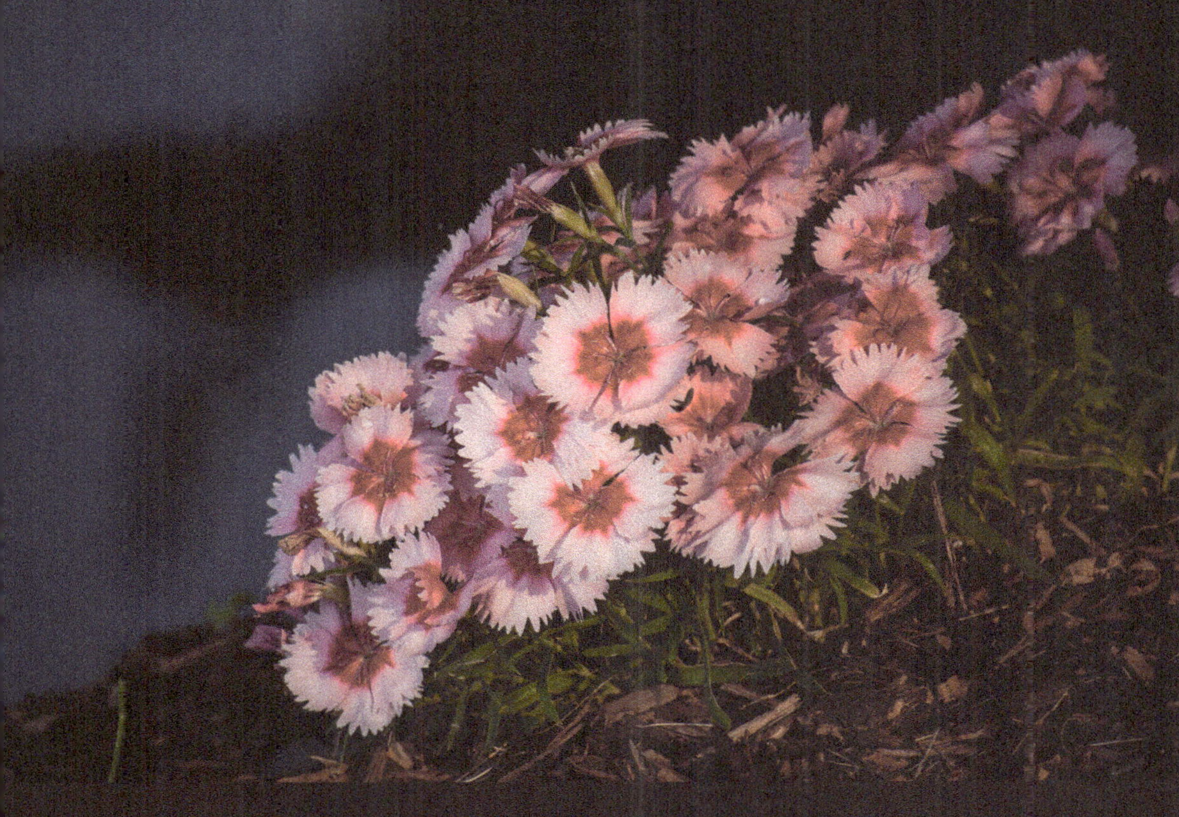

The family reunion was in full swing. When humans walked by, the flowers fell silent, not wanting to call attention. As soon as the danger passed, they cut loose, danced with the wind, laughed at silly jokes, and talked about old times.

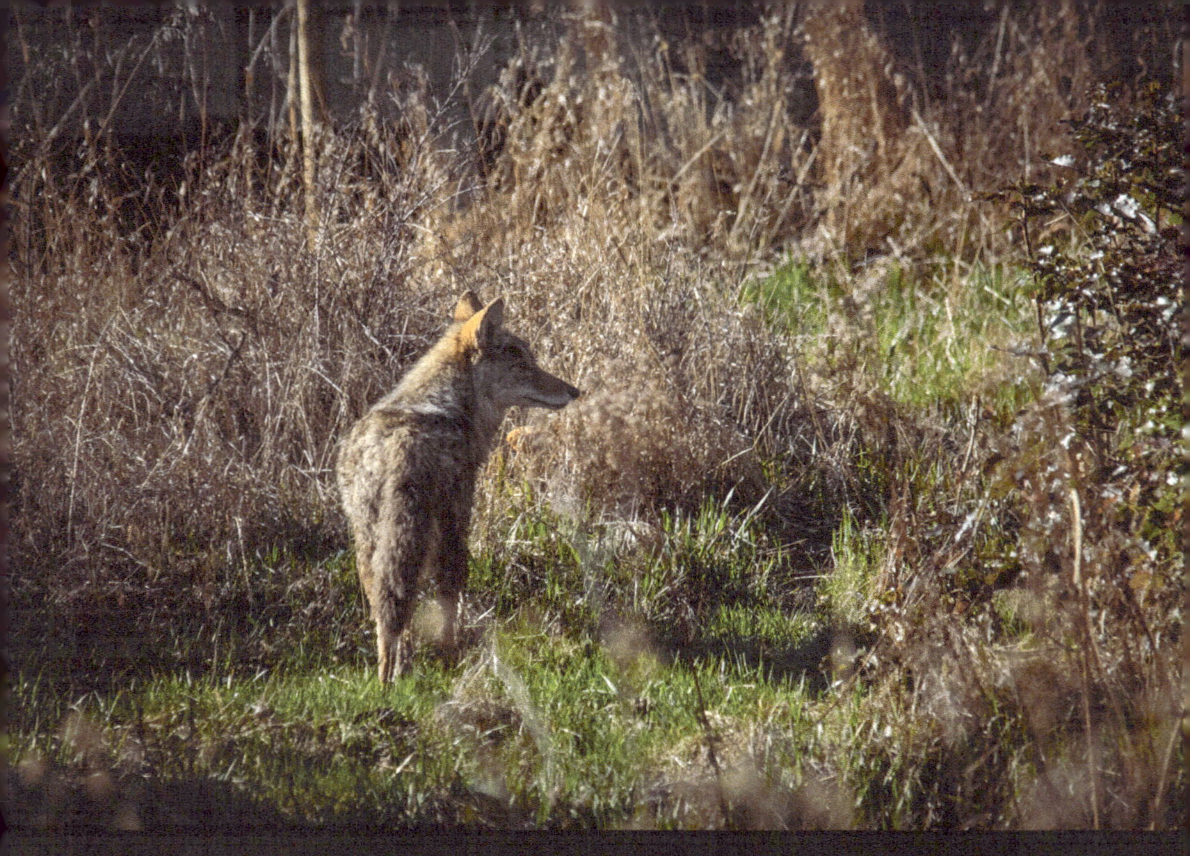

He preferred the fresh duck so plentiful in the marsh. But he answered the lure of a human's easy offer of hamburger.

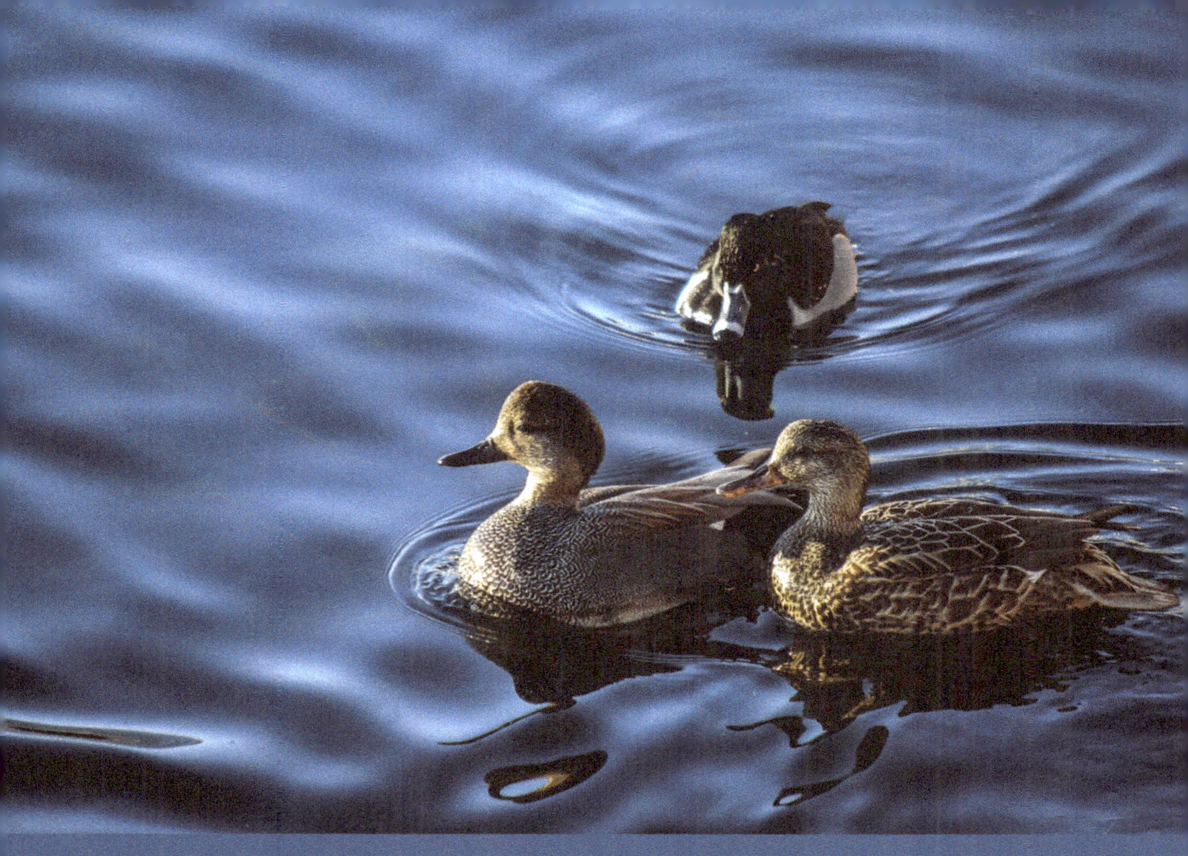

The Gadwalls were not impressed. Merganser had his eye on the female and sidled up to her. They swam away, shuddering at the thought of chicks that might look like him.

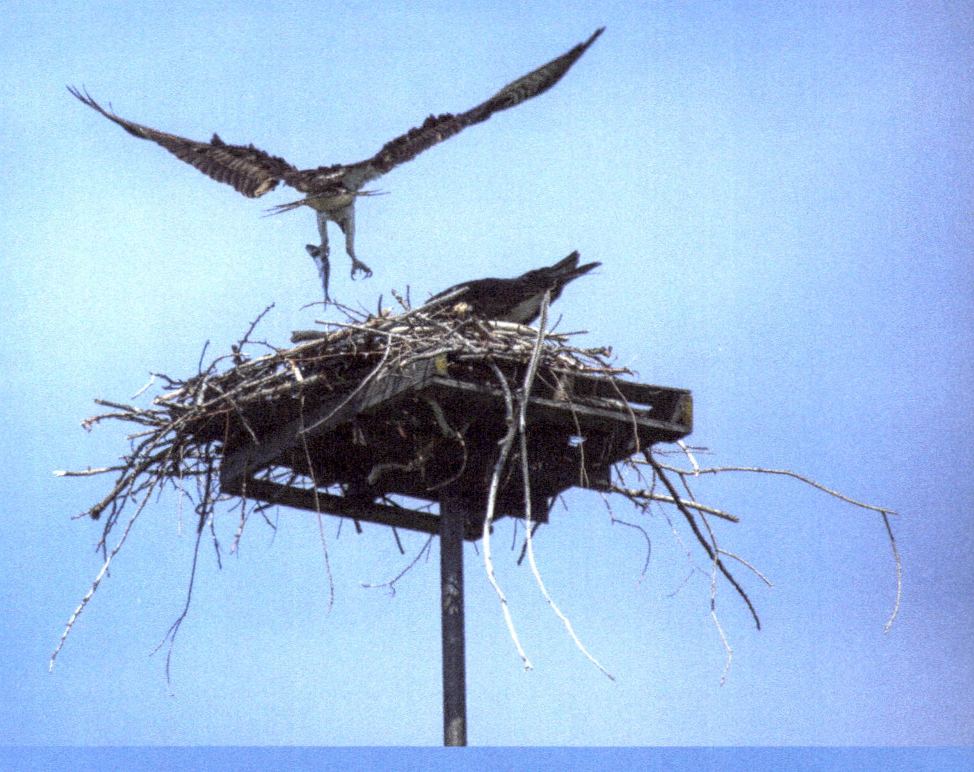

Osprey was proud to bring home a fish for his mate and their growing chicks. His sharp eyes, skilled flying, and unerring concentration was keeping them well fed. The babies would grow intro strong adults.

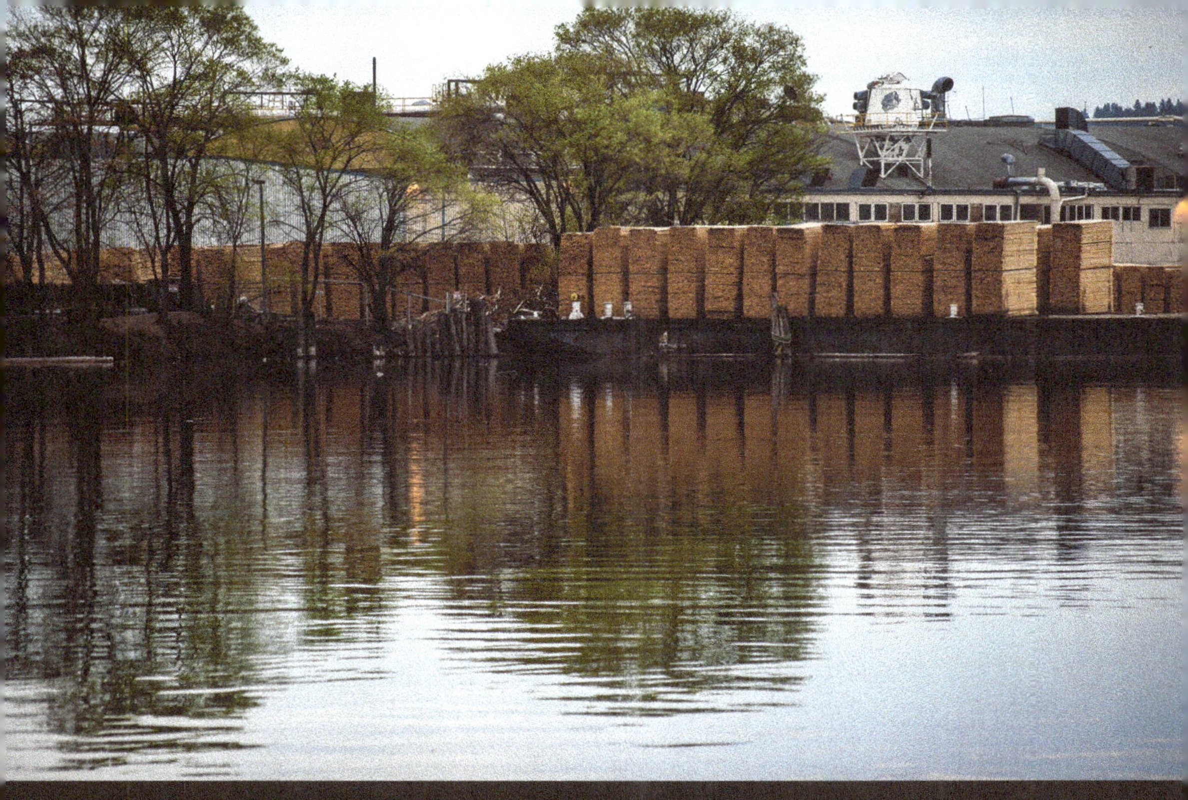

The trees waited uncertainly. They had been sawed off their roots, ripped by sharp teeth, and stacked with strangers. Rumors swirled, but they had no way of knowing if they would end up as houses or newspaper.

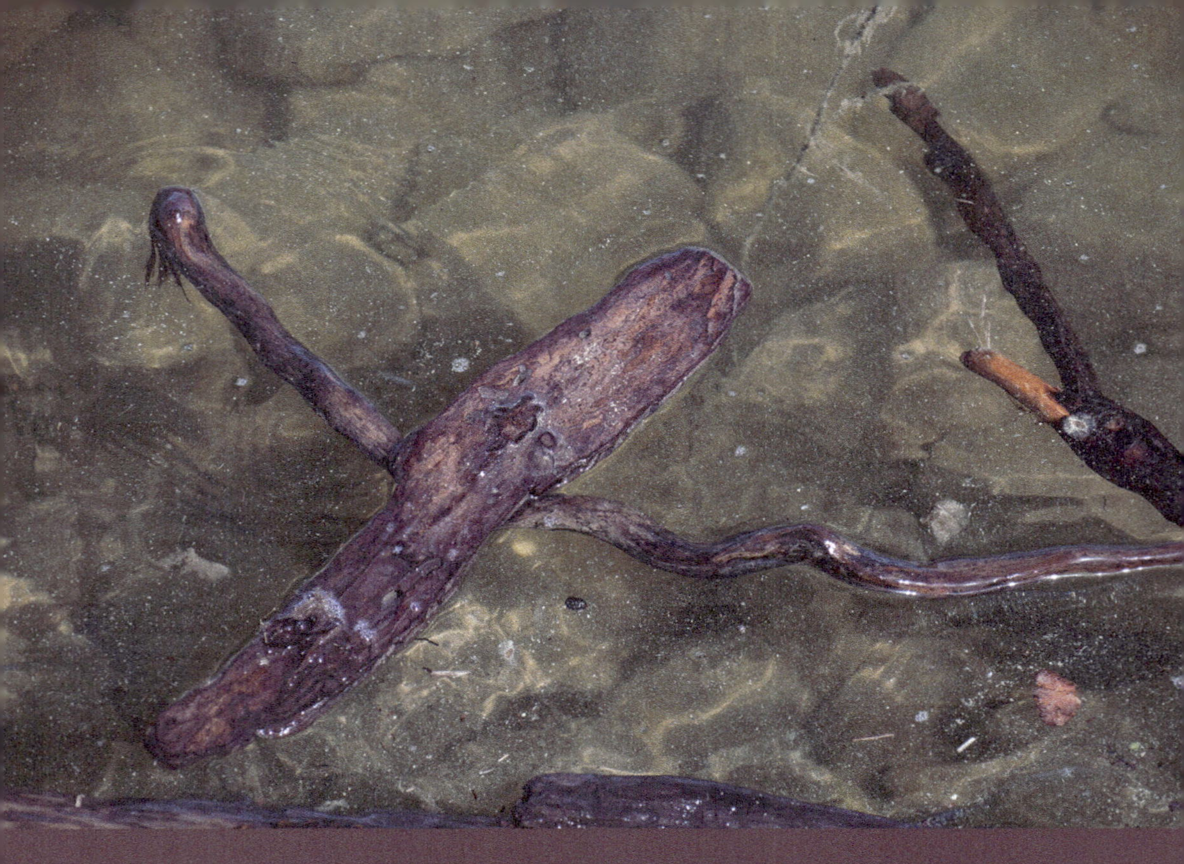

Long, thin stick pretended she was a scary snake. Short, wide stick pretended the "snake" was one of those plastic noodles children use in pools. Even though they were playing different games, both were having fun. So was Unicorn Duck.

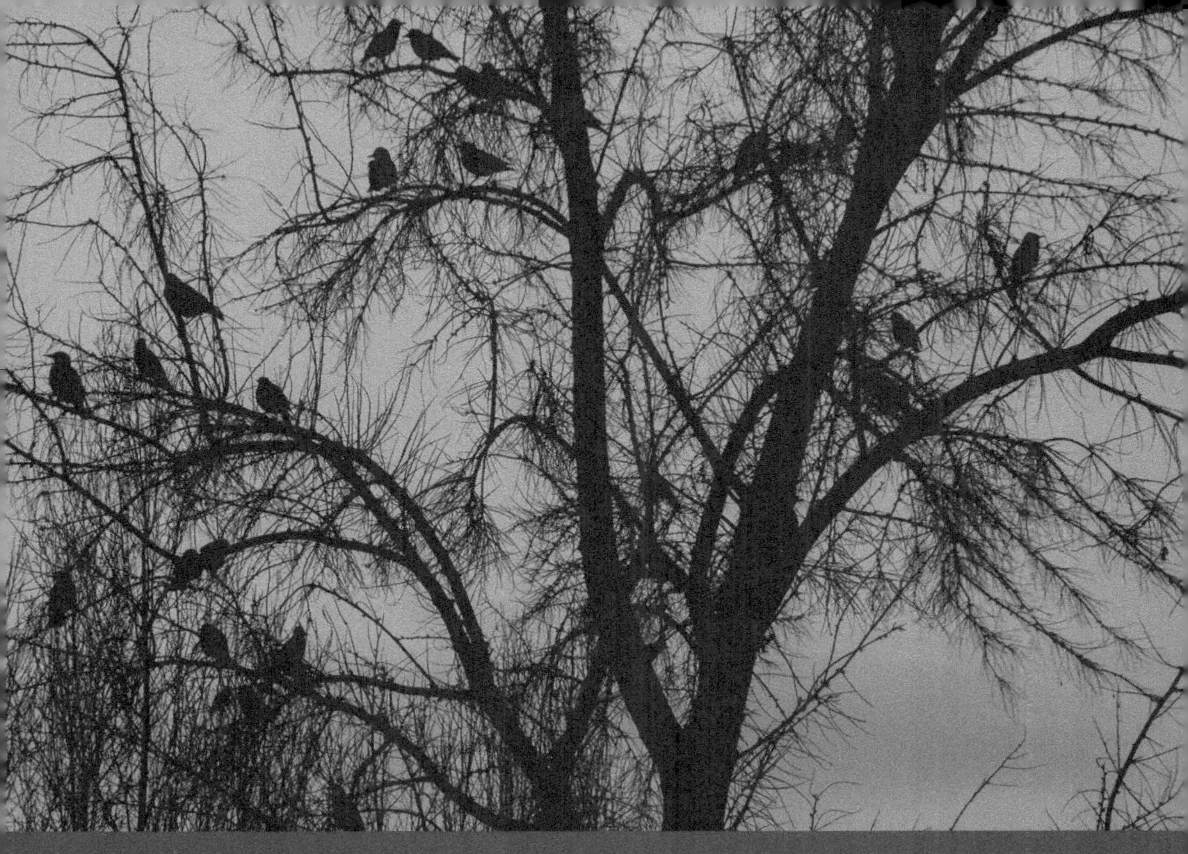

"Sing a song of sixpence, a pocket full of rye." When Jimbo came to the next line, "Four and twenty blackbirds baked in a pie," they realized 24 of them were sitting in the tree. The singing party ended in total chaos.

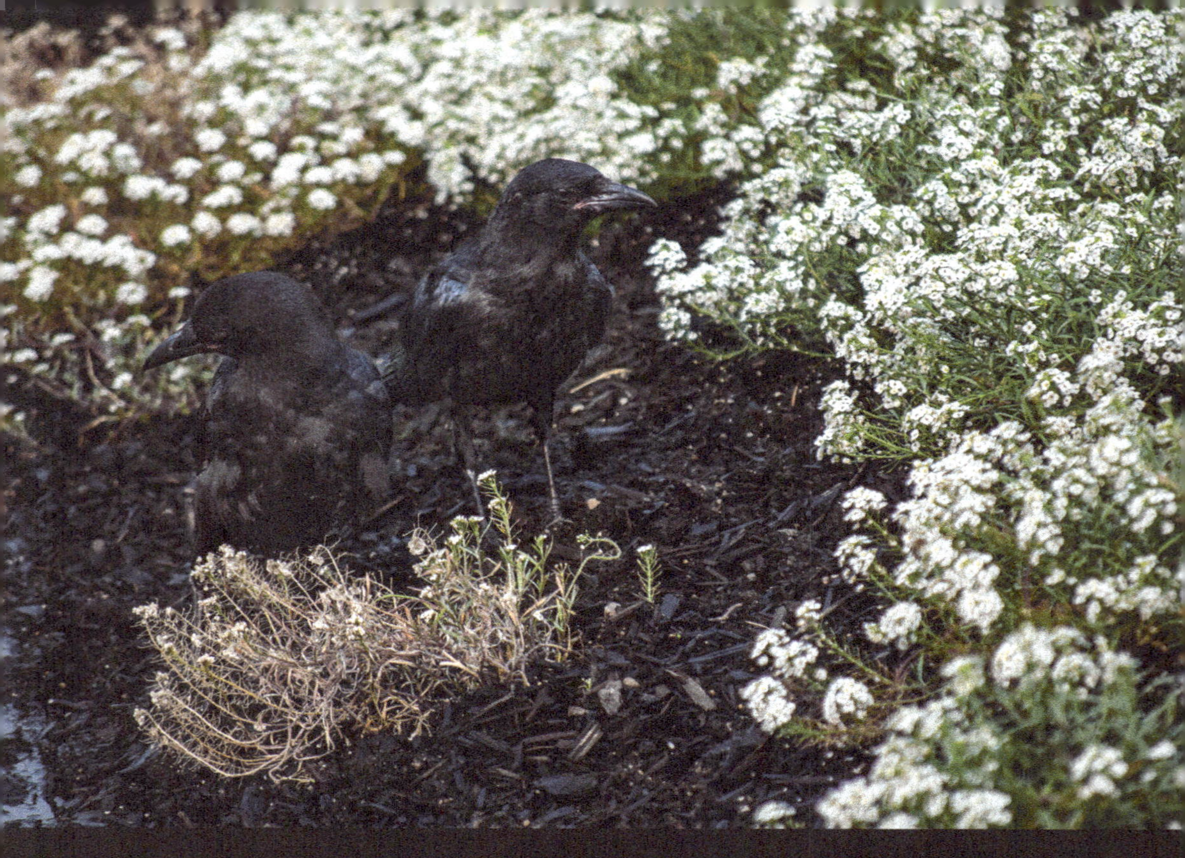

"Hey, Mac, I think she spotted us." Mac shook his head. "Not possible," he said. "Our camouflage is flawless. She's looking at the flowers."

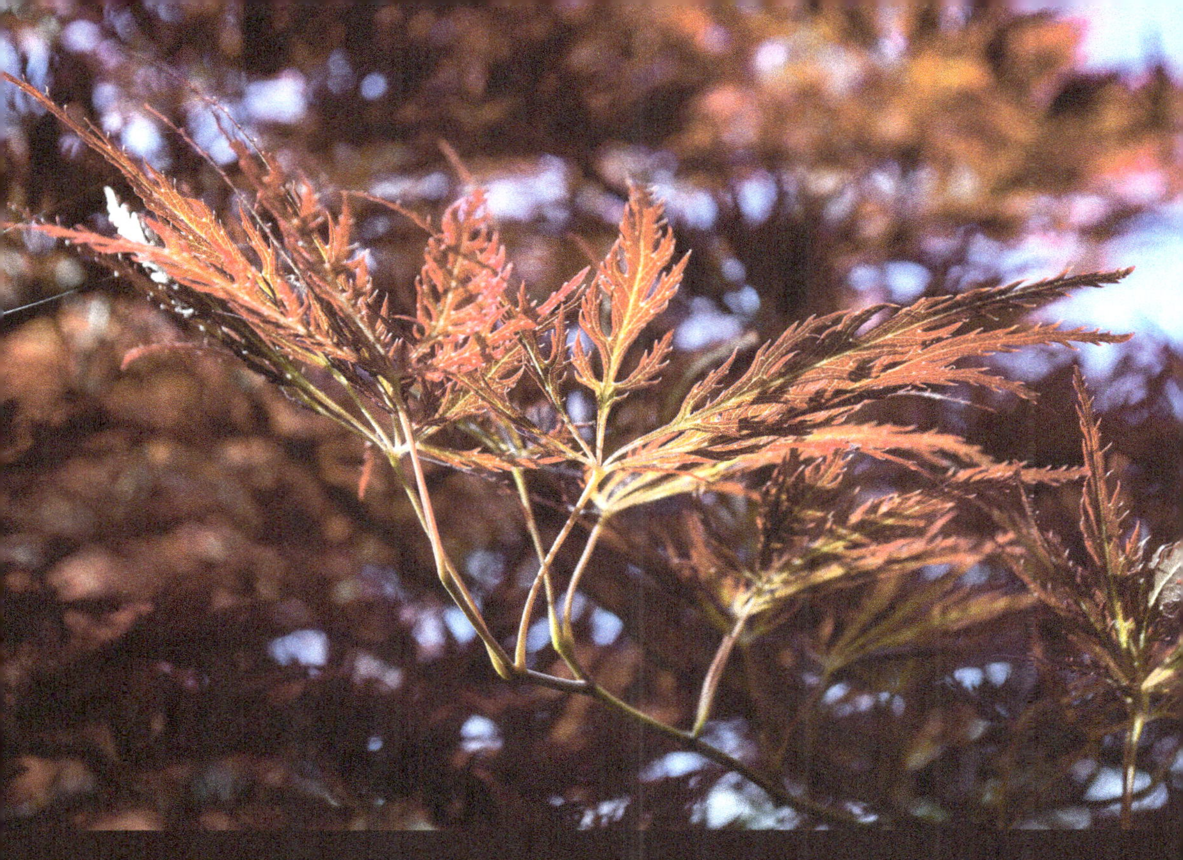

The green bushes nearby laughed at her summer dress. Their laughter would turn to awe when freezing temperatures turned their leaves to muted yellows, while Japanese Maple glowed even brighter.

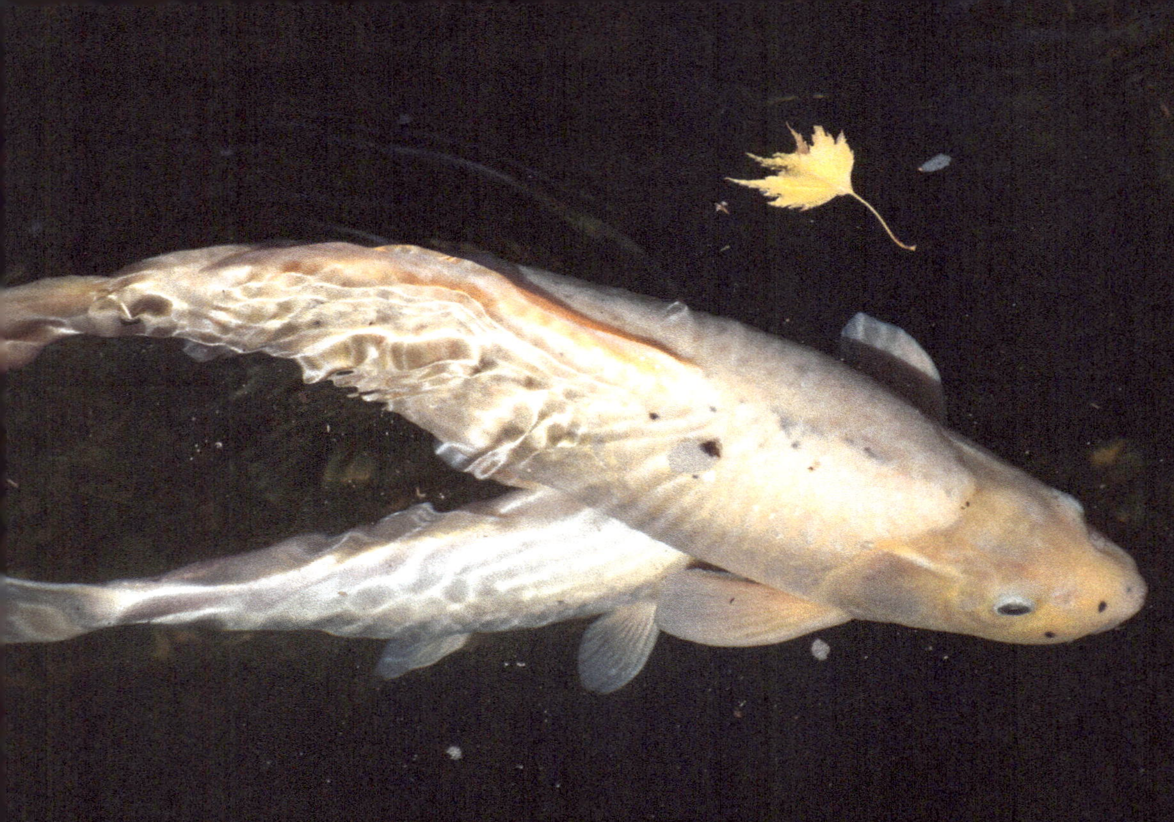

He loved to startle the big fish by suddenly swimming beneath him. "Juvenile," they would grumble, but he knew they secretly enjoyed the special attention.

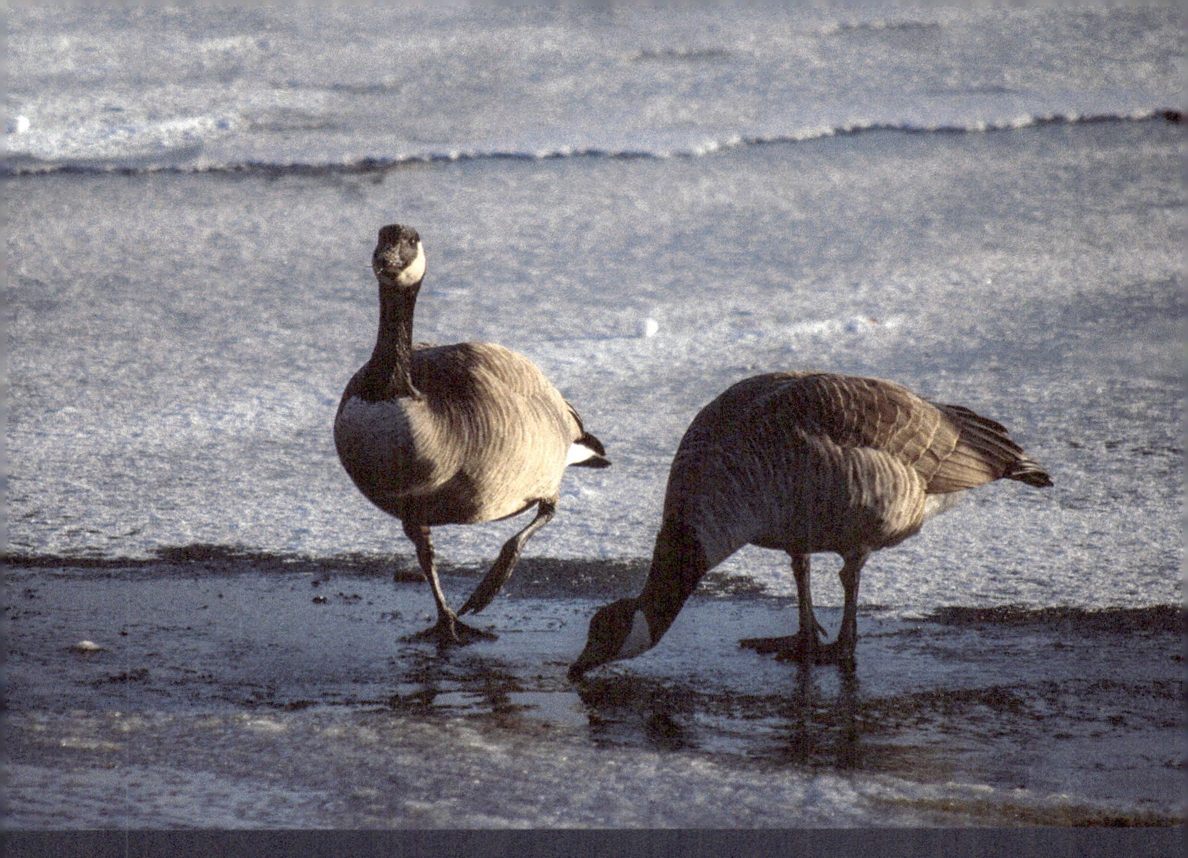

While her mate drank from what little water had not yet turned to ice, Henrietta thought about summer, eggs, and new chicks. She was beginning to regret her insistence on not being a snow bird this winter.

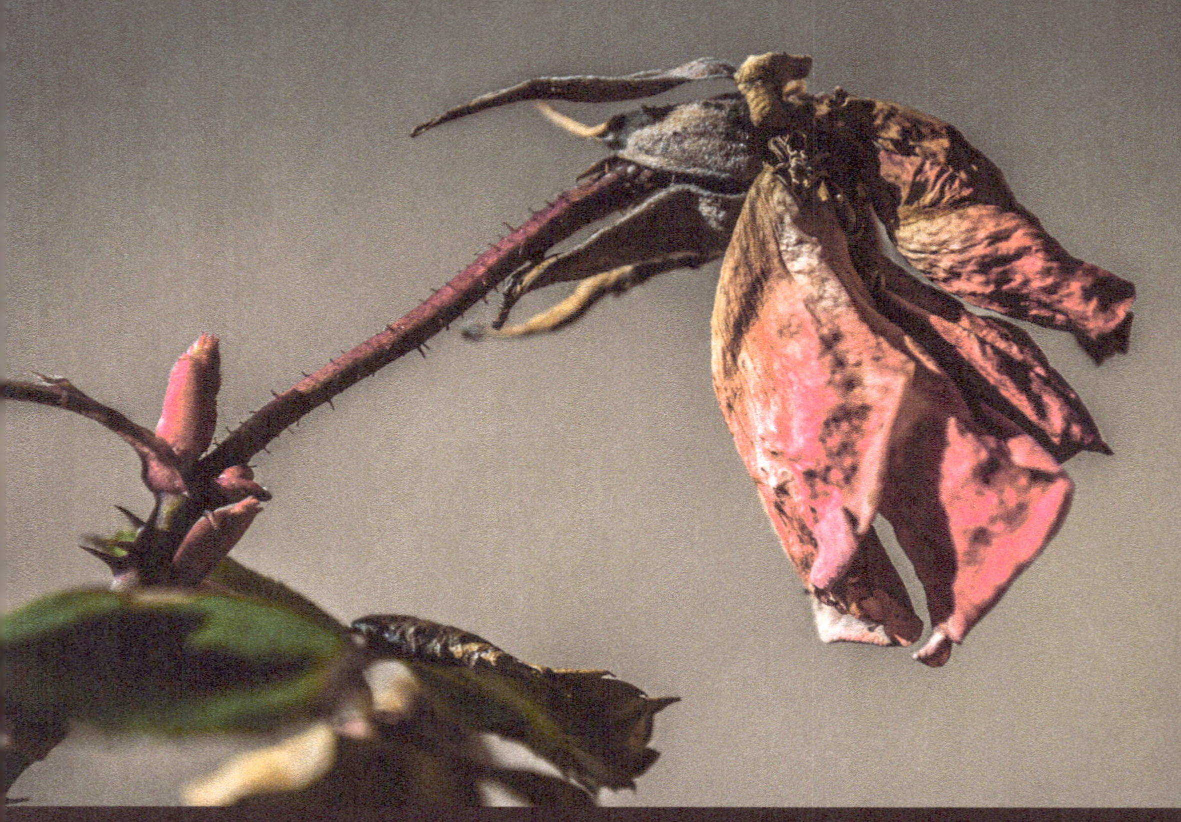

Some days, aging weighed heavily on Rose. This was not one of them, for she looked back and saw her daughters bursting with new life.

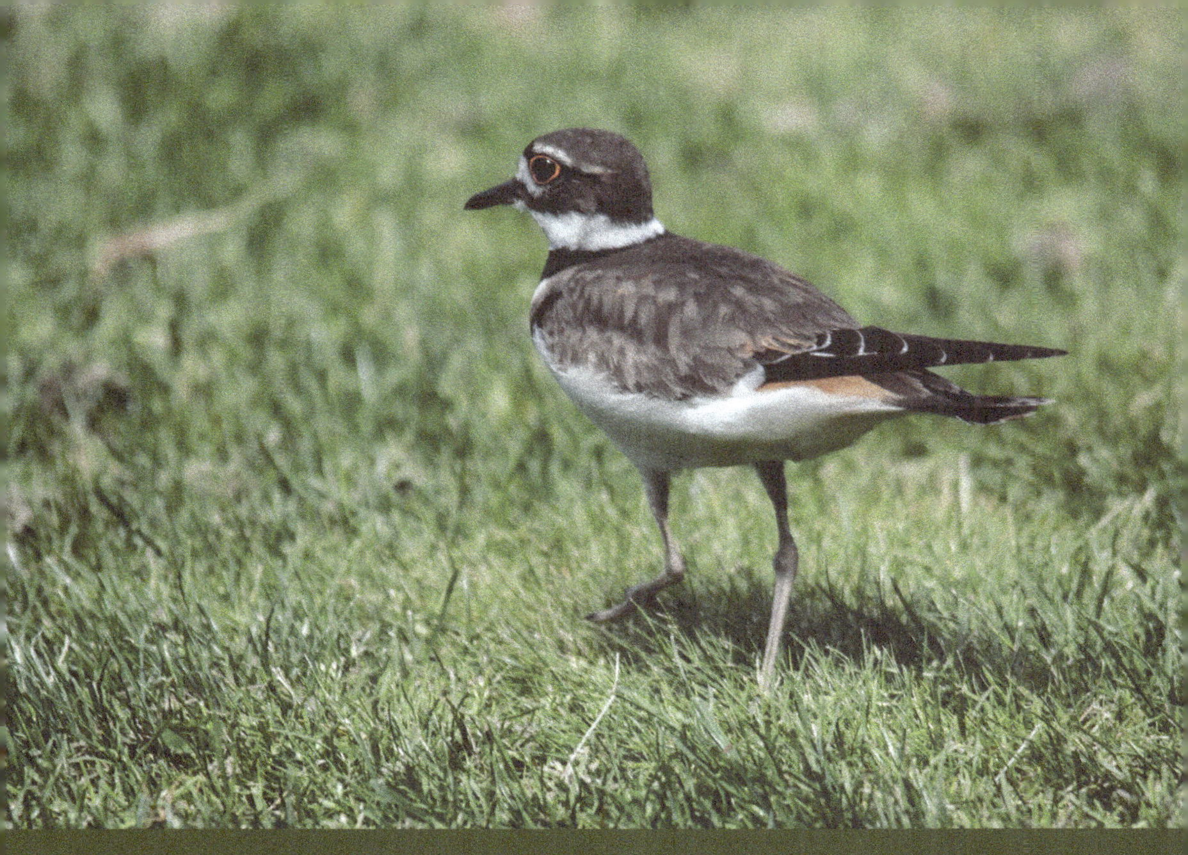

Killdeer was alarmed. Two-legged was nearing the nest where his mate sat atop her eggs. If the human came any closer, he would start his broken-wing dance and lure her away.

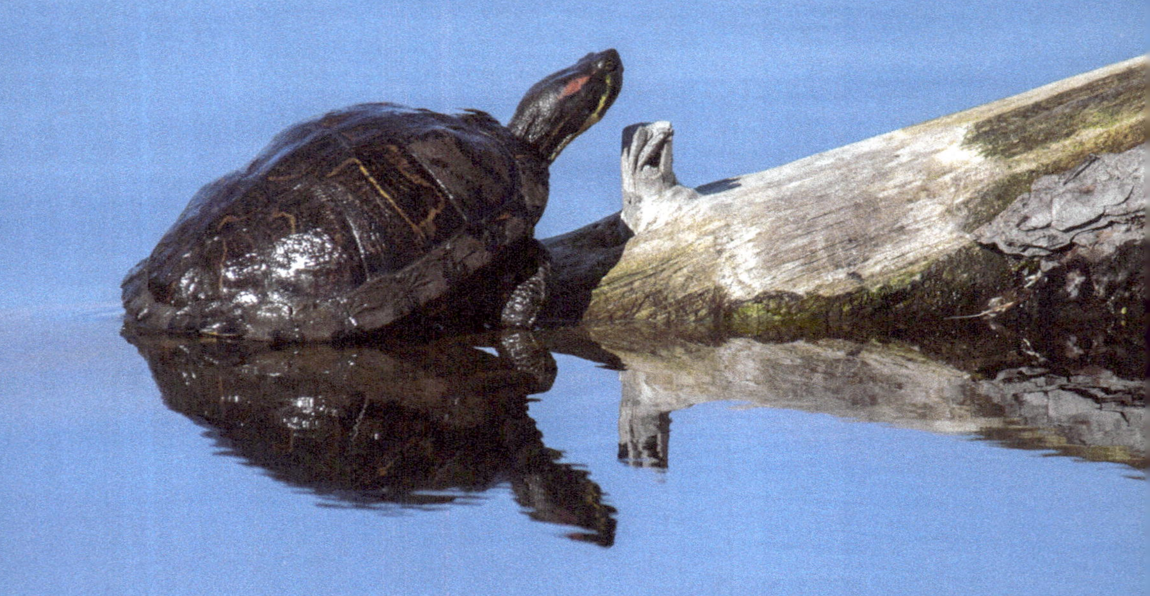

These were Slider's favorite days. He sprawled on his very own log, where he balanced easily. Sun warmed his shell, and no one bothered him.

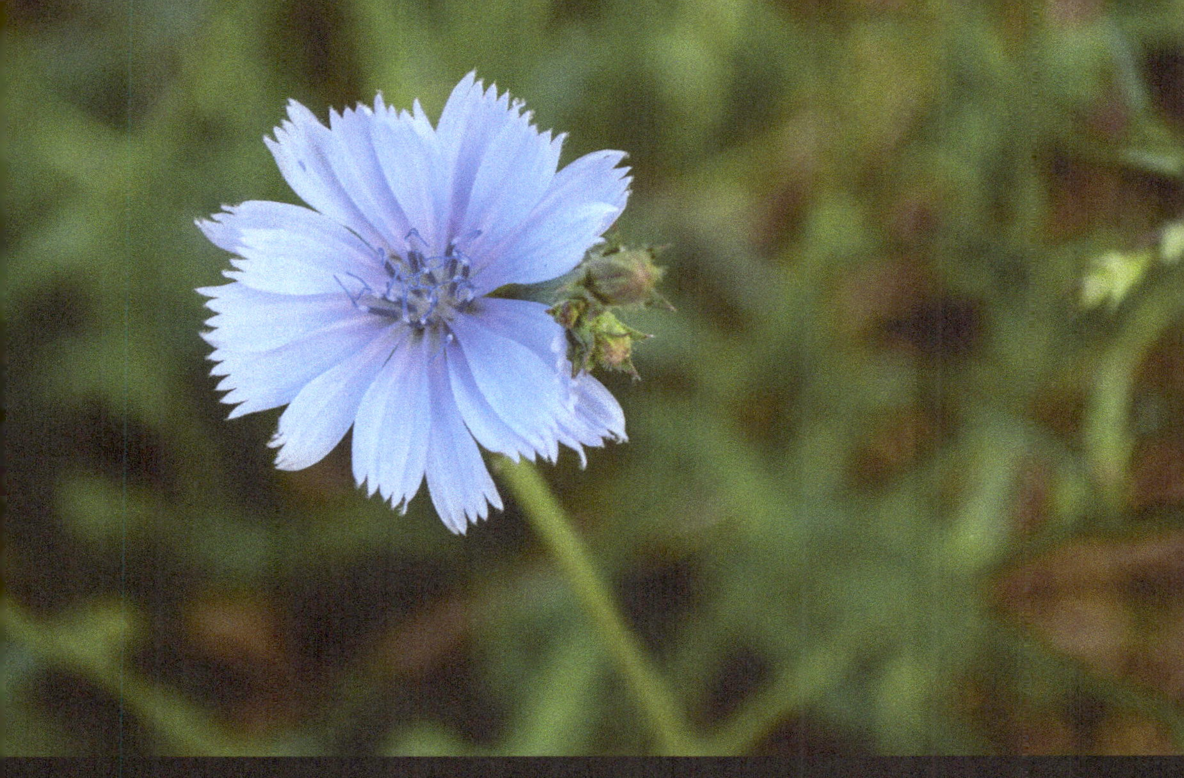

The buds peeked through her petals and gazed in wonder at the world. The profusion of green amazed and delighted them. They would spend their entire lives tethered to a stem so were grateful to have such fine neighbors.

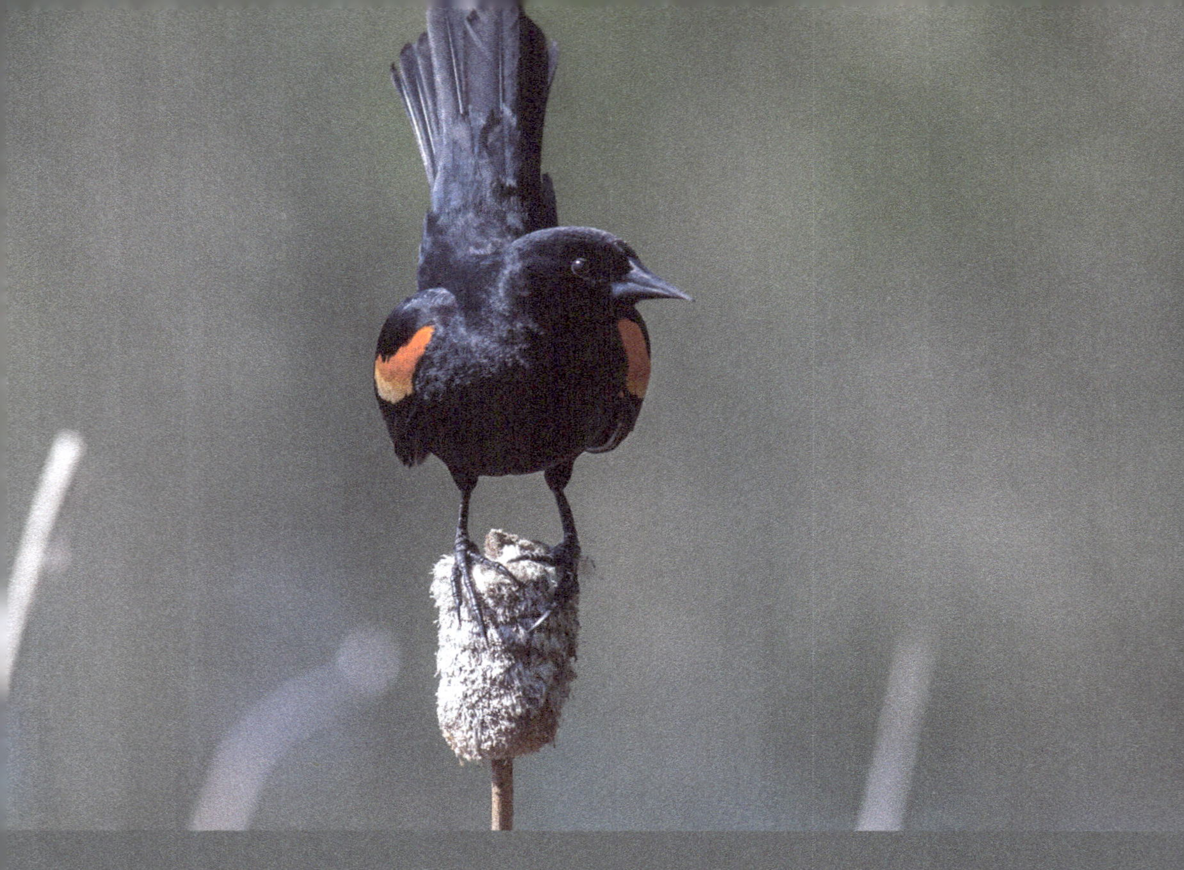

Red-winged Blackbird could not take his eyes off her. She flew gracefully, landed with ease, and paid him no attention. "Can't she see how strong and handsome I am?" he sighed.

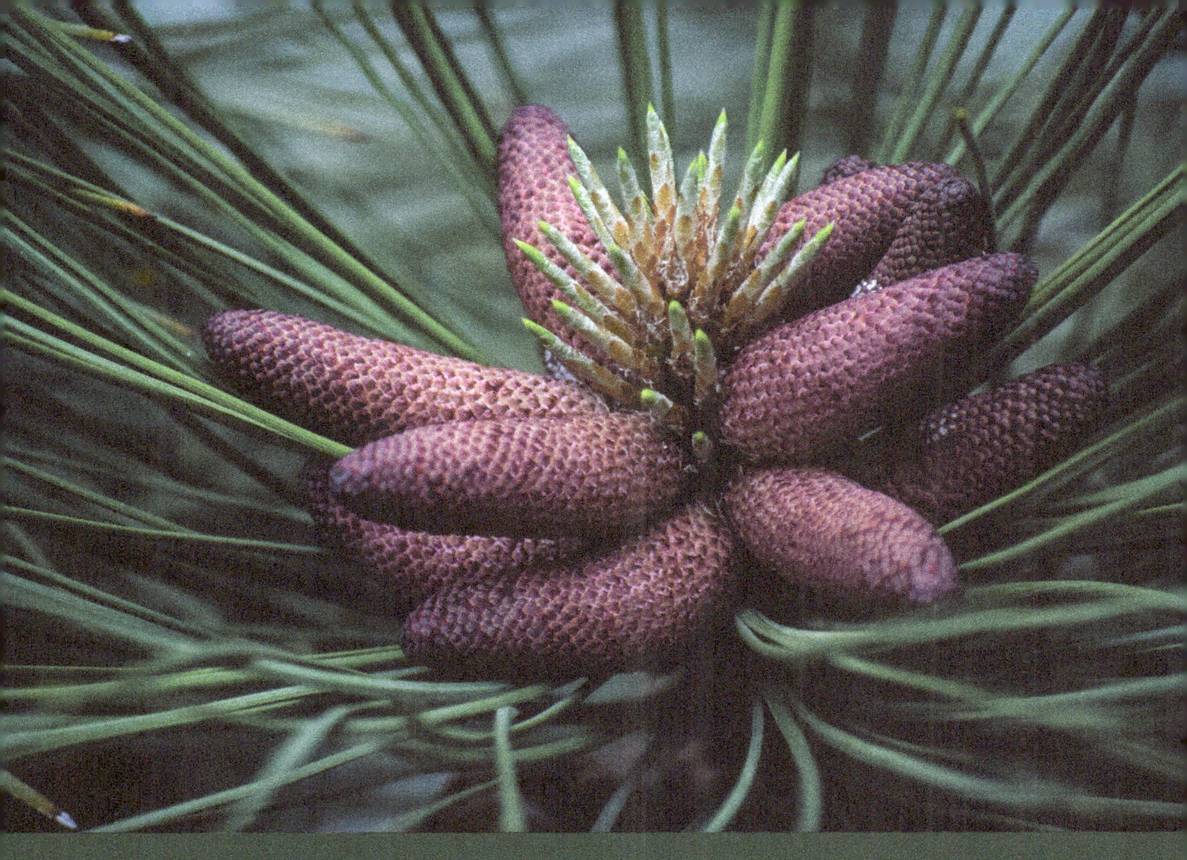

This was their first time to be pollen cones. They had no idea they would turn into clouds of yellow pollen and travel through strange lands. They thought they would always be tightly bound to each other.

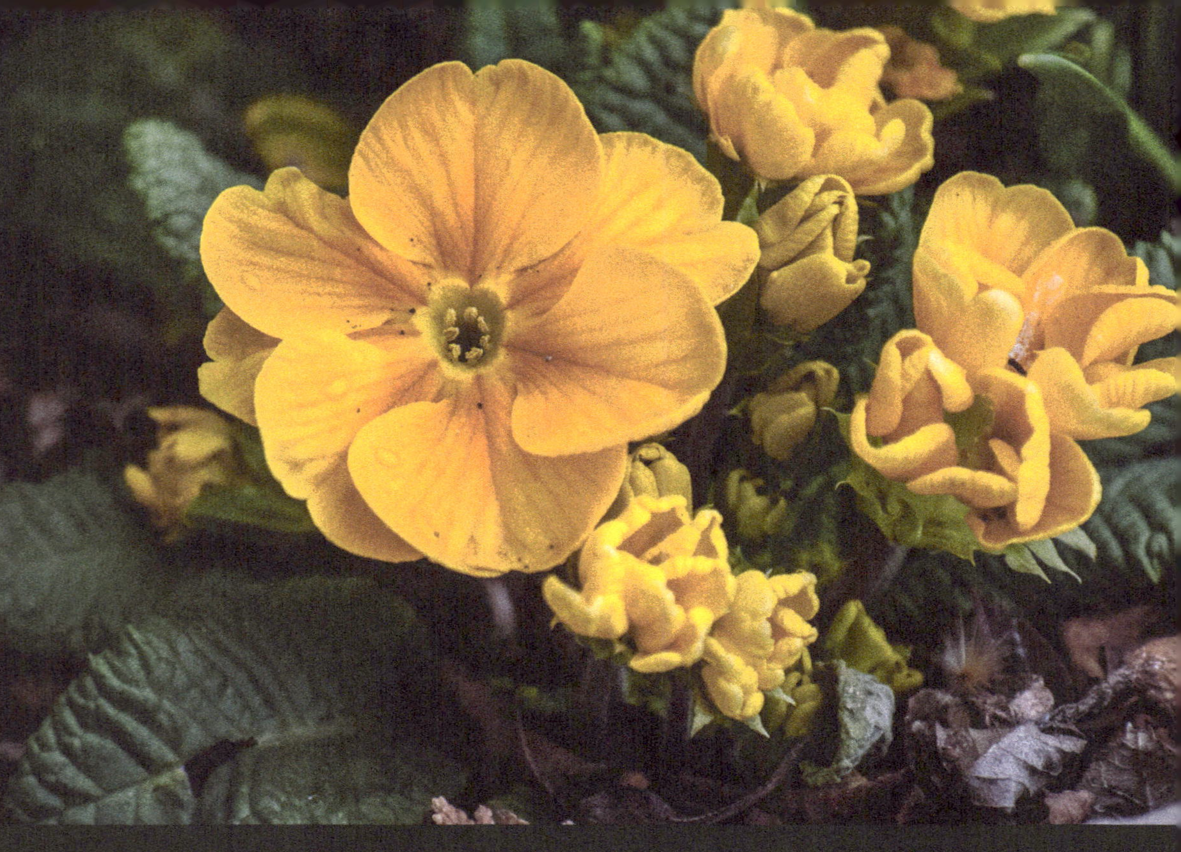

Primrose was in a hurry to open her bright face to the spring sun. Her sisters held back. They still felt the sharp night cold and wanted to wait for warmer weather.

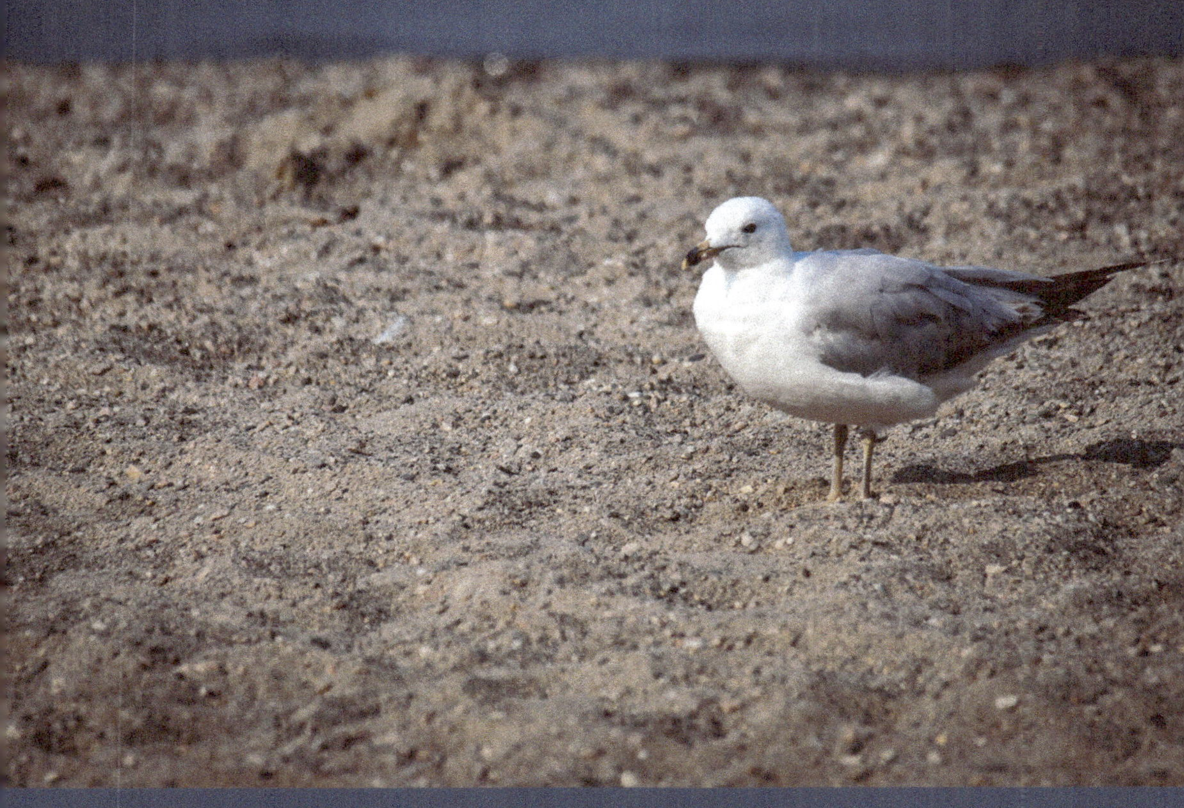

"Singing in the sand, just singing in the sand. What a glorious feeling..." Gull sang lustily in spite of unappreciative humans. He was NOT just squawking. He was singing...beautifully.

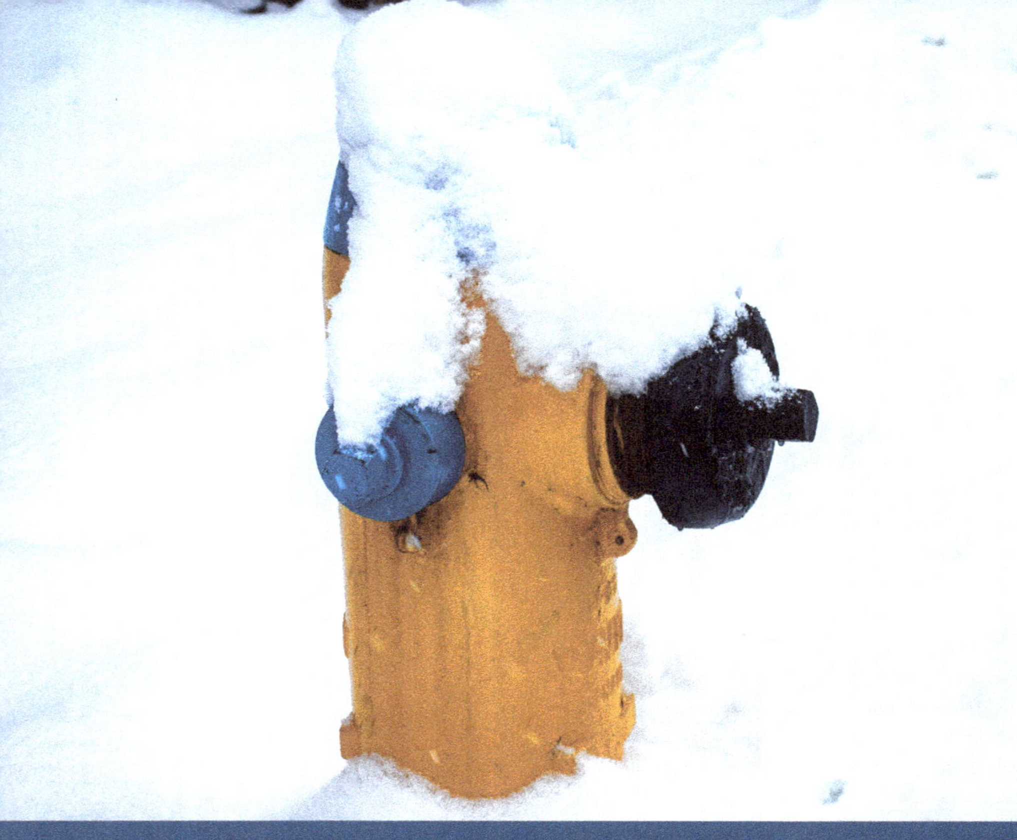

Hydrant loved snow. With a topping like this one, he played Snoopy. Only a few passersby recognized the likeness to Charlie Brown's canine pal, but those who did snapped photos. Hydrant felt like a star.

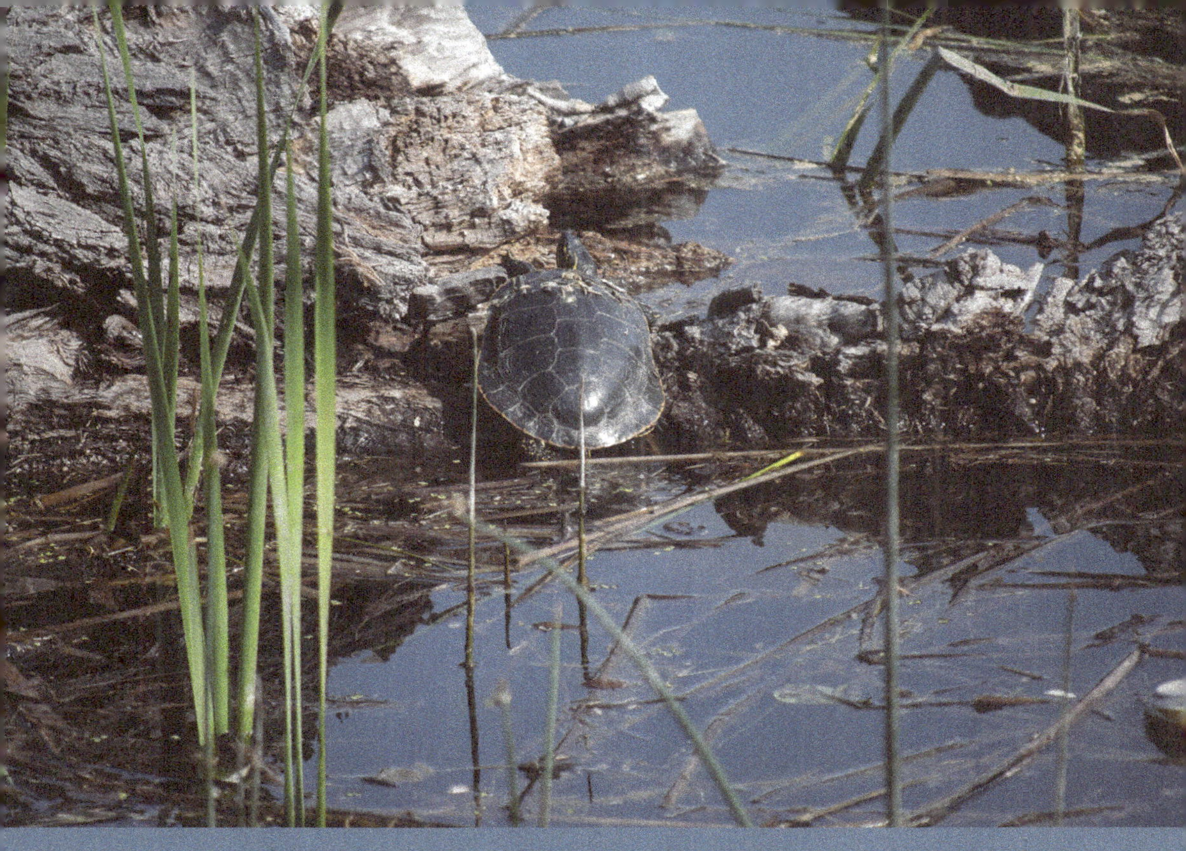

Turtle was in an unusually loquacious mood today. He looked around for someone to talk to but only saw Beer Can. "You're even more of an introvert than I am," he sighed.

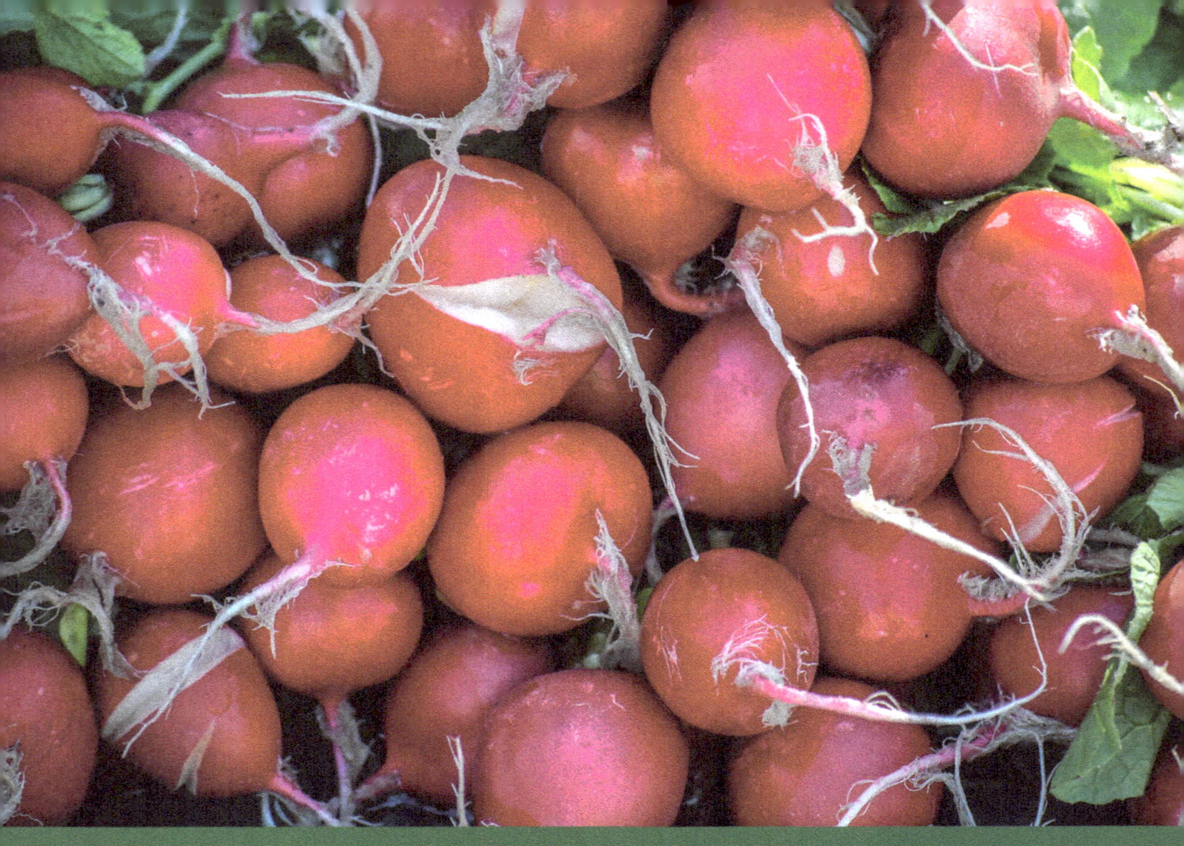

The radishes were yanked out of the cool earth and forced into crowded piles. They decided on radical action. "Burn their tongues!" they chanted.

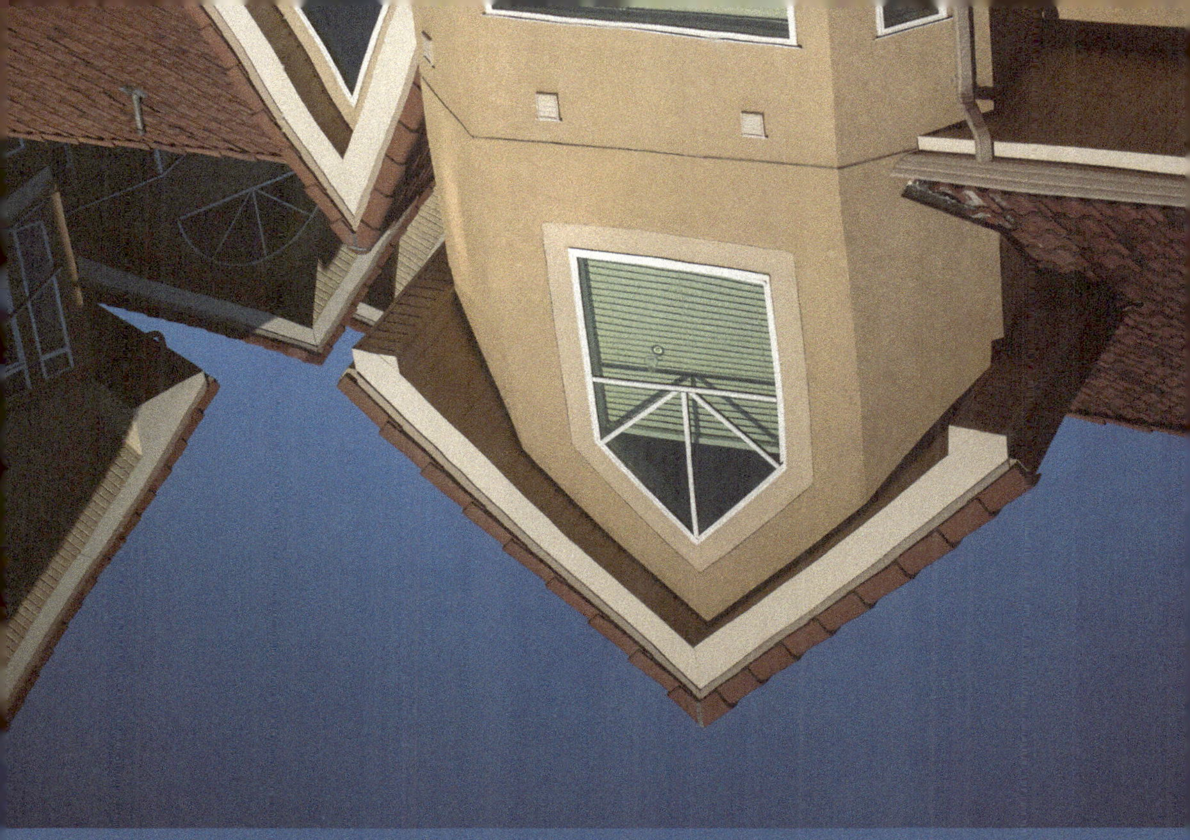

"Come on in. The water's fine," laughed Lagoon. Townhouse was confused. He was sure he was standing on dry land, but when he looked down at his reflection, he felt dizzy.

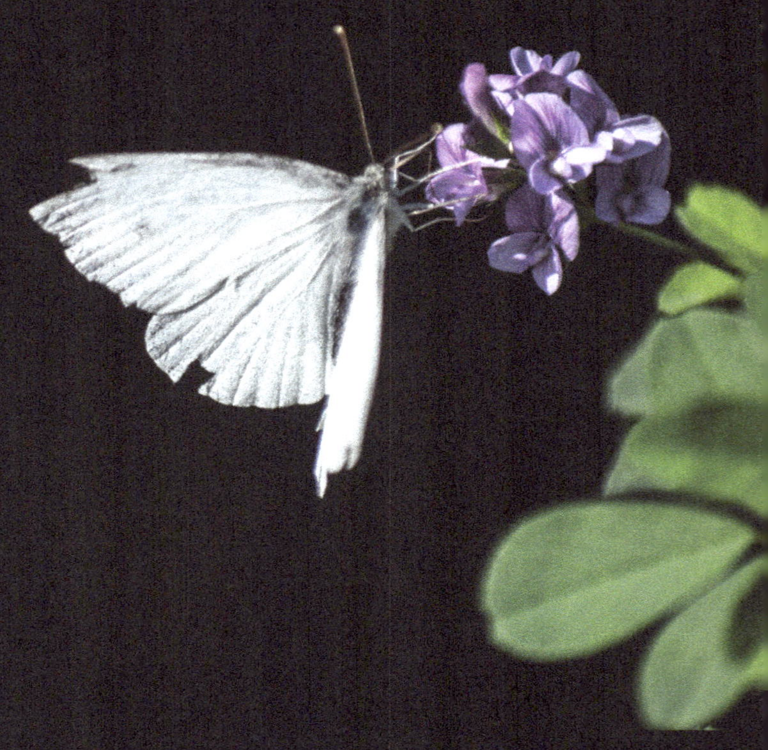

Her wings were tattered, her flight erratic, but against the deep purple of the flowers she loved, she knew she was a stunning dancer.

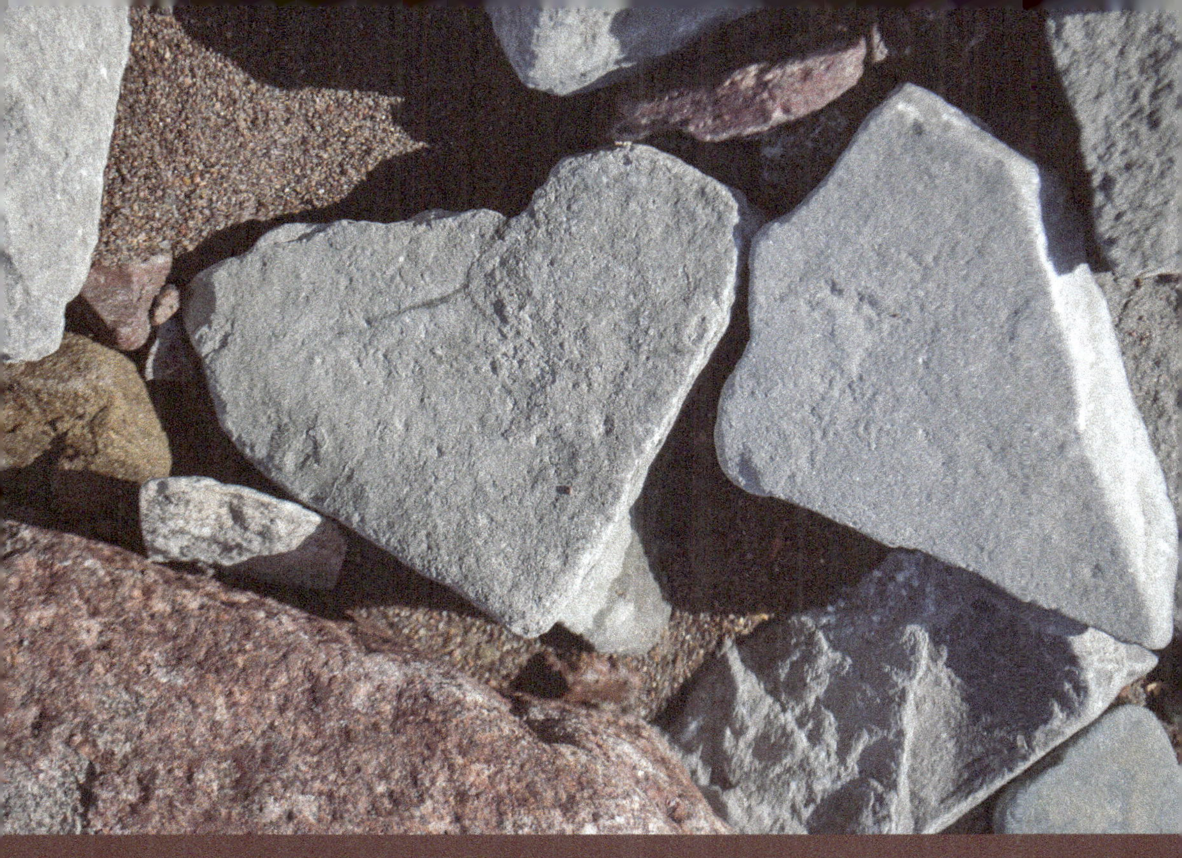

"I have a soft heart," whispered Rock, as he snuggled into the stone next to him. "How'd you like to be my Valentine?" He figured if things didn't work out, Tide would eventually bring him a new love.

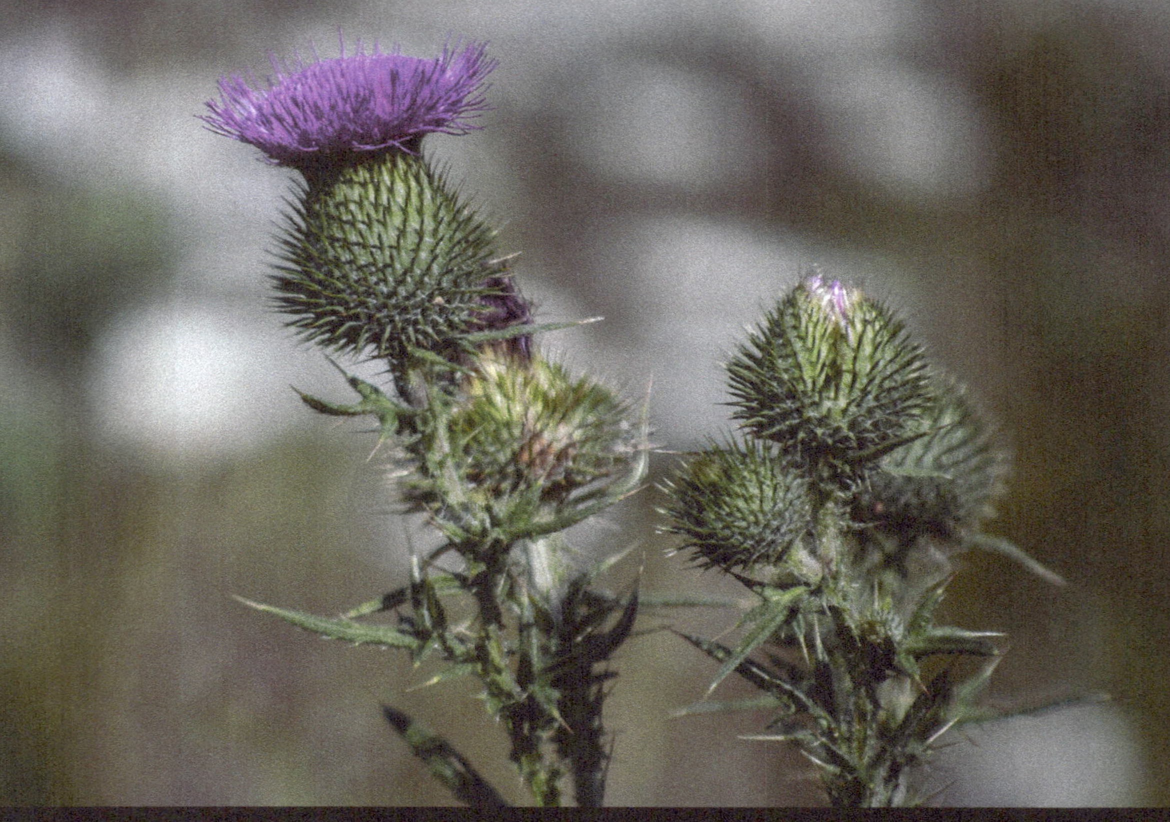

The little ones looked at her crown and longed to be just like her. The teenager, on the cusp of flowering, sneered at the old-fashioned color and shape, sure her own crown would put the oldster's to shame.

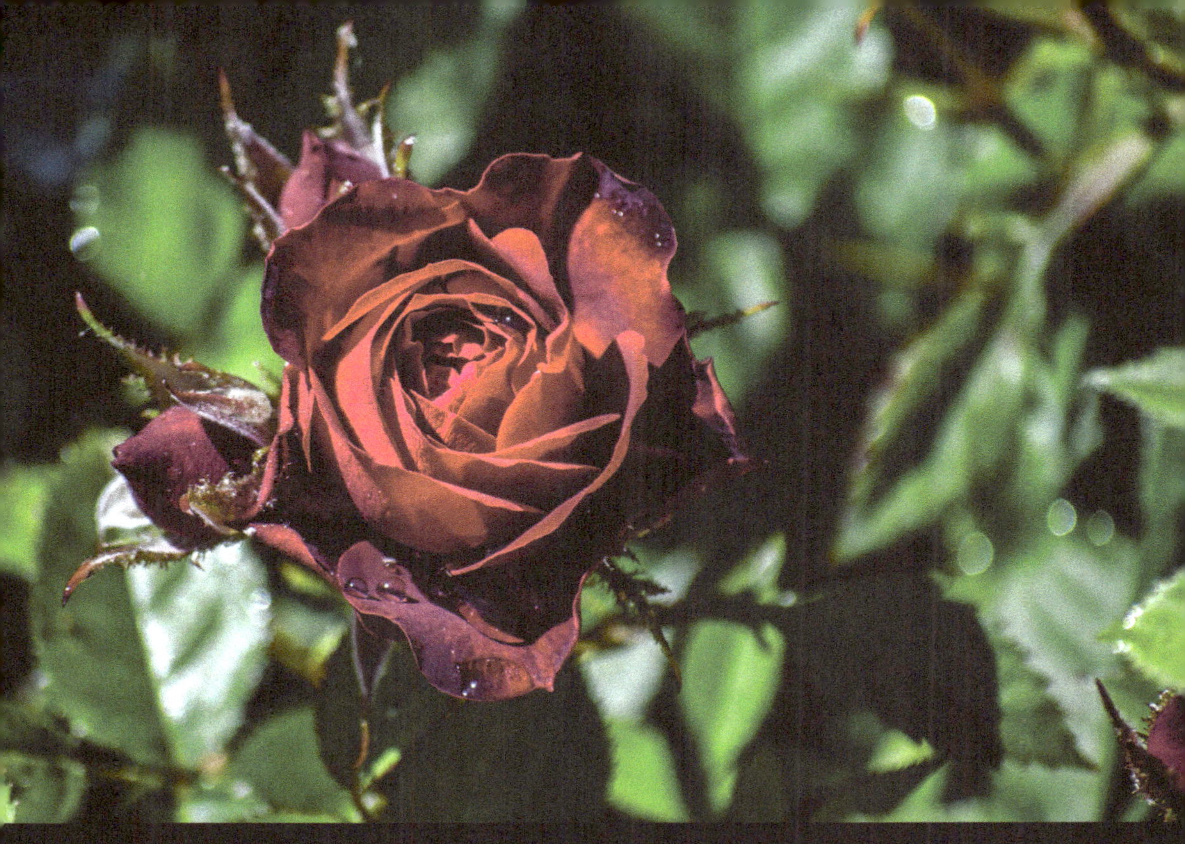

Rain kissed Rose and left a tracing of his love for her. She welcomed Sun's warmth but was sad to lose the last, wet reminders of Rain.

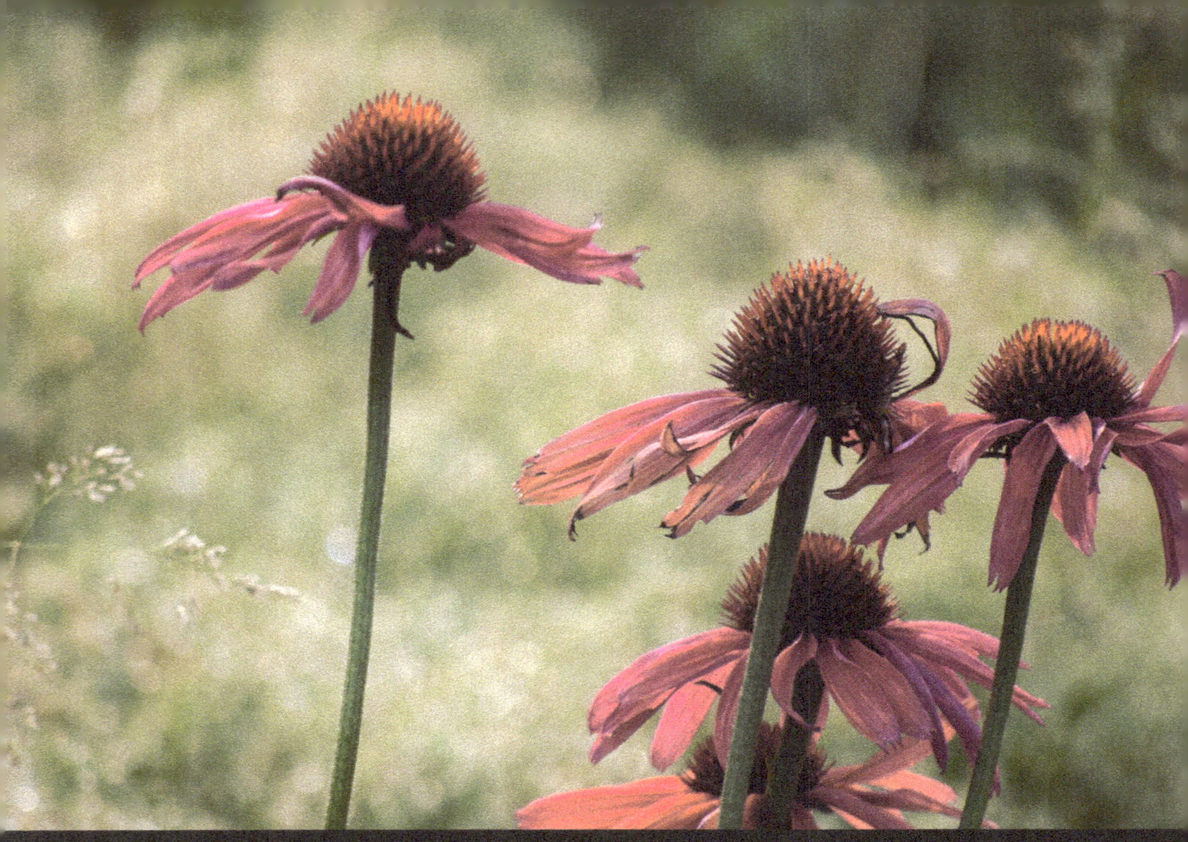

As the edges of their petals darkened and dried, the coneflower sisters practiced their farewell waves. What a splendid blossom time it had been. They already looked forward to next year.

ABOUT THE AUTHOR

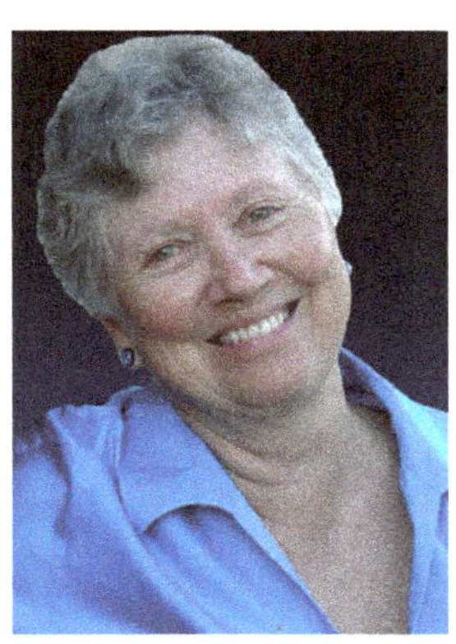

Cathryn Wellner is a writer, photographer and storyteller living in Kelowna, British Columbia, Canada. Her recent books:

In the Shelter of Each Other
The Disappearing Pumpkin Choir
That Tree Talked to Me
Parts of Me Are Still Amazing
Your Task Is to Be Admired
Hope Wins
Feisty Aging
In the Hug of Hills
Millie's Feathered Foster Family
Turkey Baby and the Hungry Hawk
Turkey Baby Finds Her Magic

You can find links to these and her other books at cathrynwellner.com. Contact her at cathryn@cathrynwellner.com or 778-478-2760. Her photographs can be found on her Web site, as well as on Facebook and Instagram.

BE A BOOK REVIEW ANGEL

If you enjoyed this book, please post a review on Amazon or Goodreads. Share it with friends and rave about it on social media. You can contact the author at cathryn@cathrynwellner.com.

Authors rely on their readers to help spread the word about books they like. People who review books are special kinds of reader angels. I guarantee when you review this book, or any other book that has given you pleasure in any way, you'll feel those wings poking out your back. Look closely in the mirror, and you might even see a halo.

Credits

Fonts used on cover and some interior pages: Saltash, Sun Kissed, and Amelia's Quill. Font used in stories: Bw Surco. Logo font: Ed's Market. Patterned edge and grunge border on cover are by Blixa 6 Studios and RuleByArt. Bear & wreath on dedication page by Lisa Glanz. All fonts and graphic elements are licensed through DesignCuts.

Text and photographs by Cathryn Wellner. The book was designed in Photoshop.

Thank you to the creative people who designed the unique fonts and elements incorporated in this book. I continually learn from you.

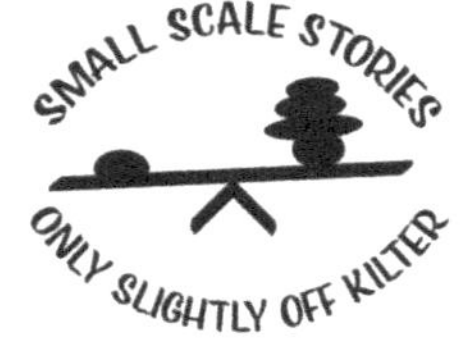

www.ingramcontent.com/pod-product-compliance
Lightning Source LLC
Chambersburg PA
CBHW041050050726
47599CB00018B/2097